THE EXILES

E. Leo Foster

The Exiles

© 2015 E. Leo Foster

Print ISBN: 978-1-48356-493-7

eBook ISBN: 978-1-48356-494-4

TABLE OF CONTENTS

CROSSING THE DEMARCATION LINE

Anny stood where the grass of the graveyard met the road's pavement. She leaned into the open driver side window as I shifted the Continental into park.

"Leave, now.... now," she warned, begging me even. "Leave." Her breath reeked from chewed up Oxycontin and generic gin swimming in phlegm.

I hesitated. I always hesitated, asking, "Why?"

When I tried to step out of my car, Anny stuck her arm straight out towards me, slamming her palm against my chest.

"Go," she said. "I'm serious."

But I didn't go. As I stepped out of the car, I knocked her hand off my chest and stood up.

My opportunity to change things, make my life—

our lives—better ended, just like that.

Just by what Anny wore, I knew something was wrong. She had on a cropped back sweater over her long-sleeved black dress, which ran straight passed her ankles, folding over itself and rubbing the ground. The bottom carried reddish brown clay caught on the silk fabric, which constantly scraped the ground.

Under a chain of grey clouds, she concealed her eyes, wearing massive black sunglasses.

I was so concerned about Anny, reaching to rip those sunglasses off her face, wanting to see her eyes, wanting to feel love just one more time, that I had drowned out the siren's screams. I didn't hear the brakes of the patrol car squealing as they collapsed on the wheels' axis. Not until the sheriff's Crown Victoria slammed into my Continental did my consciousness resurface to its surroundings.

The collision spun the front end of the Continental towards me, towards Anny, who I pushed out of the way, out of the madness.

But for me, I was too late.

The spinning car clipped my body, propelling me to the asphalt.

The sheriff tried to jump out of the Vic so fast that he tripped over himself and rolled out instead.

I pushed myself up before he did and tested my right leg, which had taken most of the impact. As I planted weight on the tender joints, Anny gave me a subtle clue that she must have been in on this ambush, even if just reluctantly.

"I wanted to trust you so bad. Why Johnny? Why didn't you trust me?"

Though a little weak, my leg wasn't broken or fractured.

The sheriff said, "Annadale, I'm so sorry baby. I didn't mean for that… you know."

I assumed right away the sheriff was Anny's father. All his apology did was just confirm my assumption. All his arrival did was explain why Anny was dressed like that.

Anny was hiding herself from her family.

"You still have a chance. Take off! Forget about me!" she yelled.

"Annadale," her dad interrupted.

"They're gonna kill you," Anny yelled. "Go."

Anny tried to balance her loyalty to her family with her love for me.

"Annadale, come over here now," the sheriff commanded. "Get away from that pervert."

How ironic? Anny's dad called me a pervert.

Her father watched as I stood on the demarcation line between the pavement and the grass, between him and his daughter, and between my past and my future.

"Why didn't you tell me the truth Johnny?" she asked again.

Anny lifted her dress a few inches to avoid tripping over it as she backpedaled away from me and towards her dad.

How was I supposed to tell her that the truth never worked for me, ever? How was I supposed to trust the truth now? People say they want the truth, but in actuality the truth is a contagious disease that nobody wants to give or receive.

It's not something you should share with people.

Standing alone, I watched Anny's shoulders sink as she dropped her head down, crying. I watched her dad embrace his damaged daughter.

Then I took off.

I hobbled up a hill, maneuvering around and across the tombstones that stood in my way.

Odd, the sheriff didn't chase me.

When I reached the top of the hill, I saw a woman standing over a fresh pile of black dirt. She stared right back at me. The woman had to be Anny's mother. I could tell. I made out Anny's features in this woman's face—her wide nose and her high arching eyebrows. Even the large lower purple lip matched Anny's.

What didn't match was Anny's heart.

Odd, Anny's mother didn't try to stop me either.

I kept limping down and up another hill that held the bones of so many people, including their secrets buried deep inside their marrow.

How times have changed.

I moved as fast as I could until I reached the edge of the cemetery. Then I walked down an adjacent street until I heard a familiar engine revving from high to low, shifting gears and coming my way. Adam, Anny's brother's, drove his sun-yellow Honda Civic right up beside me.

Anny's brother, I knew him well, and I knew his "random" appearance wasn't a coincidence. It started to make sense. When I ran away from Anny's dad without any resistance and with Mom just looking on, I felt like a lonely fox in the woods behind a high society country club. I was simply a prize token of an elaborate high stakes game played by this sick family.

They weren't just going to let me take off, not without a sinister plan.

Through the car window, Adam waved his lanky tattooed left arm back and forth. I awkwardly waved back.

"Johnny, dude," Adam yelled ridiculously loud. He pushed his vocal cords hard again. "Get in. We both got to get the fuck outta here."

Just ambushed by Anny's family, I was confused.

"Why?" I hesitated and asked, "Who?"

If Anny would betray me, then Adam definitely would.

They both hated their father, but for different reasons. Despite that hatred, their father was still blood, and I was still an outsider no matter how close I had gotten with them.

"Listen dude, my dad knows about you, about Brookings, about the murder," he said. "I'm telling you the truth."

Curiosity killed the cat. Well, curiosity was about to kill me.

"I have a plan," he said, and I wondered if his plan was to kill me or save me.

I hesitated. I felt if I ran away and kept running, then I would never know what's going on, what's their plan, and I would never see Anny again, so eventually I stepped inside his Civic.

"Forget them," Adam said.

As I was about to find out, it wasn't me trying to forget his family. It was his family that had a plan on forgetting me, just like everyone else that came into my life.

MEET THE HAYDENS

To understand what I was up against, I need to tell you about the Haydens; well, most of them anyways. I need to tell you about their connections and resources, so you'll know I never really had a chance, and that the idea of a second chance doesn't really exist due to all the Hayden types that are out there.

Anny's family reminded you why another crack at life is an illusion after you make your first big mistake.

Her family represented the people who make sure your past stays connected to you.

They ensured every mistake you made remains consequential for the rest of your life.

Anny's dad was a sheriff who had access to a national clearing house called NCIC, which maintains accumulated data about you and everyone else in America. This information ranges from every petty traffic violation you committed to the property you once owned. And he didn't just have access to this database; he was certified to enter information about anybody in the databank as well. Anny said he used to brag about it too, telling her if he couldn't find dirt on people, then he would just enter in some made up shit on them, like how they conducted an act of bestiality on the side of Highway 41.

Then there was Anny's aunt, who worked at Equifax. As an analyst, she monitored real time credit activity on everyone. If she was curious about you like she was about me, then she would research all your spending habits, including all your accumulated debt- and just like that she knew you.

If her aunt and dad didn't have enough access to your "personal" life, her mother was a private detective. She would put your entire past together. She worked for clients such as federal law enforcement agencies and law firms. Her biggest client was Krutz and Montgomery LLP, where they paid for her access to databases like LexisNexis, another data collection company holding way too much "personal" information about your life. With this access, she would know everything about anyone's legal history, including liens, alimony, bankruptcies, or any petty reason why anyone had to interact with the government. However, Krutz and Montgomery only provided her with databases to public information. What made Anny's mom special were her connections to insiders in agencies like the FBI and CIA. She was connected to several of these agencies' employees, who were willing to sell her all kinds of confidential information about anyone, including me.

Whether you actually committed a crime or not, whether you were found guilty or not, a record of your alleged immorality exists forever, both as a public record or as a piece of confidential data, which can be easily purchased for the right price.

Because of people like the Haydens, your past always lingers with you. If you made a mistake, then your character will always be questioned today, tomorrow, and even after your death. It might have only been an allegation, a rumor, but that rumor will become you.

Trust me, you can't escape it. Types like the Haydens will catch you.

THEN THERE'S ADAM

Adam said his family was, "hypocrites, all of them."

Adam lived off this hypocrisy.

"We, and I mean society and the government dude, say no to drugs, yet we all smoke and shoot anything, any damn pill, that will let us sleep better, or will give us energy, or quit makin' us stress, you know—help us concentrate, you know—whatever. But here's the thing. We're all beggin' for something, but unless a doctor prescribes it, we're not allowed to consume it."

According to Adam, telling a doctor about your symptoms meant you're telling your insurance company about your symptoms, "which meant if law enforcement ever had 'probable cause' on your ass, then you're giving the police your medical history. And… and if the police accuse you of a crime—not convict, but just accuse—then your medical history is filed in the courtroom. Shit, you might as well just let everyone know what the fuck's wrong with you now. Just tell it. If you got herpes, shout it out proud," Adam ranted. "Remember, a court record is a public record."

Adam was the alternative to the doctor.

"Can you believe it? We need permission to get some relief from our fuckin' lives."

He was the guy we paid extra to keep those parts of our lives private.

Economists will tell you that we pay more for heroin, marijuana, cocaine, meth, and whatever because of the cost associated with trading and transporting these drugs by illegal means.

"Bullshit," Adam would say. "Marijuana, cocoa leafs can grow anywhere under delicate supervision by anyone with a green thumb. They can be sold by anyone too—a cartel leader or a soccer mom. It doesn't matter," Adam preached. "We're paying more for the privacy dude, to keep our 'bad habits,' our addictions, off the grid. Think about it dude. You can buy Cialis over the phone from a random pharmacy residing wherever and keep this type of drug use out of the insurance company's records. But if you need to get your hands on Adderall, then you must personally visit your physician."

Adam explained, "Who cares? Nobody's embarrassed to admit that they have trouble concentrating. But who wants to admit that they can't fuck?

"Lawmakers are the number one boner pill buying professional class in the country, inching just ahead of television anchormen dude. Look it up. These legislators were not about to let their erectile dysfunctions be vulnerable to public ridicule. They weren't taking any chances."

With this perspective, Adam justified his profession.

He was a criminal.

Despite his dad's occupation, actually because his dad was the sheriff, Adam dealt drugs for a living.

It made even more sense that I would join his criminal enterprise at one of the most vulnerable moments in my life. And it made even more sense that Adam would contemplate betraying me at another vulnerable moment of my life.

THE RIDE, PART ONE

Adam peeled down the paved road with the windows rolled down. The breeze flapped open his unbutton collar shirt, forcing the ends to fold over on themselves, revealing his Aztec serpent chest tattoo.

Adam reached over my lap, opening the glove compartment. With his left hand steering, his right hand pulled out a zip lock bag of white pills, speed. His fingers wrestled through the open bag now placed on his lap, trying to pinch a pill between his finger and thumb. He caught three pills molded together, stuck together from being stored in the humid car for days.

He shoved them in his mouth.

While crumbling the sour pills between his teeth, he offered to share his stash.

I declined and asked, "Adam, what the fuck is going on?"

Adam put both hands on the steering wheel and drove through a parking lot of a boarded up Blockbuster and asked, "How do you know Annadale?"

He made a hard stop, forcing some of the wheels' rubber to rub off on the asphalt.

Adam dropped his forehead on top of the steering wheel, moaning, "How'd you meet her?" He clawed his fingernails into the side of his neck until burgundy blood rushed to the skin's surface. "You're fucking her, aren't ya? Don't fuckin' lie to me."

"Damn it Adam, tell me. Tell me now. What's goin' on?"

Adam lifted his head up and looked at me with his watery blood-shot eyes. His squinting eyelids told me he was betraying me. The closer he squeezed his lids together, hiding his dilated pupils, the more I knew he was wrestling with the idea of killing me.

He said, "My mom, my dad… they know everything, dude."

I asked, "What's everything?"

He asked, "How do you know my sister, Annadale?"

"Anny," I said.

And he responded, "Annadale?"

THE DARK PLACE OF SALVATION

What Adam's family didn't know was what Adam did know.

Adam knew all about the zombies, the ones living underground, in exile. Their names didn't appear on those databases that his father and aunt relied on. They avoided government; it didn't matter what happened to them. If they were robbed or beaten, they didn't call the police; they had their own system of justice—revenge. These people lived on the periphery of society, not in it. Adam knew about the dark places they roamed. He knew about these places and the people that only took cash. He knew about the duplex rentals that filled their vacancies only by word of mouth rather than through rental listings. He knew that in this world, landing a good job didn't require a background check or a credit check. He knew your resume was worthless here. He knew your past didn't carry the same amount of stigma and scrutiny as the "plugged in" world. And he knew that my only chance for survival was here in the underground.

Prior mistakes didn't measure a man's worth in these places.

These people relied more on the devil's good graces than prayer. These places resembled hell more than Mayberry. But here, I had freedom like never before. Here, I had a chance to escape my past, rewrite my life, and Adam knew this.

But what Adam still didn't know was how I met his sister Anny.

A HAPPY BEGINNING

When I walked inside Tokyo Spa, I didn't even pretend anymore. I didn't even pretend that I didn't know what full service meant.

Society pretends though; Adam taught me that.

In the land of the free, we pretend that we outlaw prostitution because "we the people" morally object to the oldest profession. Yet, over eighty percent of spouses cheat on their marriages—half of which pay for a prostitute to do so. The real reason prostitution is outlawed is that so many of us, the Johns, don't want our indiscretions recorded? If sex were a legal business, then sex would have to be regulated, which then means every transaction would have to produce a receipt.

"A record must exist in case Prostitution Inc. is sued, audited, or filed for bankruptcy," Adam preached. "Then your sex transaction will be a public record."

Prostitution works both ways, though.

If you're a lady, or a man, wanting to make great money, but don't want to file taxes and don't want to be connected to the grid, then illegally selling your body can work. People choose these "off the reservation" professions all the time to avoid being found, to disappear from everyone, or to reinvent themselves.

Anny's motive was control.

On the grid and under the scrutiny of her father, she was powerless. Out of the sight of her family though, she gained and enacted power over the desperate, the sexually inadequate, the ones begging for love in the marketplace, and me.

What she wanted was control over her daddy.

But without a viable way to make this happen, Anny settled for the alternative, the John.

Anny took control over her clients, both the walk-ins and the ones that made reservations for the half hour massages.

This was how I met Anny.

I became her walk-in customer, directly and confidently asking for the full service, no hesitation, no signs of embarrassment vibrating off my tongue. As Rebecca, the short Cambodian front office assistant, led me to the back room I started unbuckling my belt.

"Let's make this quick," I said, assuming she was my massage therapist.

When Rebecca swung the door open, I was pushing my pants down.

Then I saw Anny, draped in a long white lab coat. Her pinewood eyes burst when she saw my boldness. She quickly tried to conceal her shock, but she was too late.

"Make yourself comfortable…if you haven't already," she said, turning towards the counter holding the trey of lotions.

I told her, "What's the difference? A happy ending, a happy beginning—it's practically the same thing but without the bullshit that's wasting both of our times."

I kicked off my shoes and pulled my legs out of my jeans.

I demanded control.

She faced me and laughed. She told me, "I bet you make a lousy fuck."

I said, "Ain't it obvious. I'm having to pay for it." Sitting on the massage table, I stiffened my arms, locking the hands against the bed's edges, forcing my triceps to pop, to bend my skin outward.

She laughed again, and then berated me some more, saying, "You're so arrogant for being so worthless."

She rubbed my shoulders. With her insults, she forced the tension to break through my tense muscles. I let go. I fell backwards. My back landed on the stiff fake leather mat.

She said, "You think you're clever cause you got a few jokes."

Then she squeezed the surfacing stress resonating just under the skin. She broke it apart, causing it to dissolve through my bloodstream.

"But they ain't laughing at your jokes. They're laughing at you."

Anny fought for control. She slid her hands under my briefs, gliding her lotion-soaked fingers over my growing member.

"How's it feel knowing if you die, nobody would give a fuck?" she asked. She grabbed my member, forcing it to stiffen up. "Huh? Tell me. How's it feel?"

She squeezed my dick so tight, I could feel the blood pumping against her grip. I told her, "It feels good."

"Tell me, tell me again, louder."

She leaned her body over my chest, letting her cleavage extend beyond her lab coat through her half-unbuttoned white jacket. I smelled the lingering cigarette residue oozing from her pores, breaking through the thick Chanel #5 shield she sprayed on to mask it. Her hand got painfully tighter as the lotion dried into my cock, turning her hold into a Velcro grip.

"It feels good...pain." I could only speak one syllable at a time.

Her fingers rubbed the skin off my dick—painful, but it was the pain I had been begging for my whole life.

"Do all of us the favor, off yourself… now, you fuckin' perv."

Anny was in control.

My dick was raging hard, barely holding in all of the frustrations, all of my built-up regrets. All of my self-loathing pumped through my member, ready to be set free- finally.

I was society's ultimate victim, but like a victim, I blamed myself.

I had begged for this—a true happy ending, where I can absorb a real pain, a punishment severe and worthy enough to forgive myself.

If everyone abandoned me, it must be my fault.

Everything I hated about myself migrated to my cock, forcing Anny's hand to widen as my dick expanded. The skin surrounding my dick had stretched extremely thin towards the climax, so thin that the pain increased.

Over and over, a callous on her palm scraped against my shaft.

At last, I could free myself of the guilt, knowing I paid my dues, knowing I felt a true pain, rather than just this numbness.

"Drown yourself in an ocean," Anny whispered in my ear, flicking her tongue on my lobe. "So we don't have to clean up your fuckin' mess."

What more did I need to endure?

"Sorry," was the only word that I pushed out along with my tears the cum that flowed out and over my dick's head like lava. My guilt slowly oozed over my shaft and over Anny's clenched hand, which had rubbed me raw.

When everybody believes you're evil, including your own mother, you start to believe it too. Even if you didn't do the actual crime that they accused you of committing, you start to believe you deserve the punishment anyway, if not for the crime, then for purely existing.

Anny told me through the climax, "The only way to change is to kill yourself." Then she grabbed my testicles. "Or...if you got the balls to do it, you can kill everyone else... Then nobody can stop you from becoming what you want to be."

THE RIDE, PART TWO

Adam's right foot pushed the gas pedal, and the Civic shot out of the lot like a cannonball.

"If it was between her and me, who would you choose?" Adam asked.

Now on the road, Adam didn't slow down for the railroad tracks ahead. Hitting them at sixty miles an hour, our heads smacked the car's ceiling, forcing our eyes to close and our chins to sandwich against our chests.

"Choose?" I asked back.

"Were you just using me to get at Annadale? Were ya?"

"That doesn't even make sense," I said.

Adam's insecurity kidnapped his logic.

He said, "She is always the favorite…always."

He dragged me into his sibling rivalry. Driving down the road, Adam saw me as his dad, turning me into the man that had neglected him all through his childhood. Right in front of Adam, his father gave all his love to Anny while never acknowledging he even had a son.

This was according to Adam.

Role-playing was easier for him. It was cathartic for him. Adam could kill me without hesitation, without remorse. He could pretend to murder his loveless father while avoiding the repercussions that would come with actually doing it.

Love and hate can mean the same thing, especially when you're referring to family.

Knowing the stakes, I said, "Adam, just stop and think for a minute." Adam leaned forward towards the windshield, arching his back. "Remember? Chad? The Church? Do you really think I went through all that shit to get with Anny?" I asked.

Adam kept staring straight ahead, not turning once to look at me, not even slightly. He visualized that I was his father sitting in the passenger seat. Seeing my face would ruin his attempt to turn this nightmare into a fantasy.

He knew the power of visualization, but unlike Adam, I knew the brutal consequences that can also come from visualization.

"Don't do something you're gonna regret," I pleaded.

REHABILITATION

The moment Chad Brookings shoved me through the Presbyterian Church's back door and rolled my body down its steps, I knew the only way I could survive was in exile.

Chad let me know it was time to embrace the worthlessness that my life had become. When you have nothing worth risking, when nothing matters anymore, you're completely free, nothing binds you—not money, not family, not morals.

This realization of my new freedom is how I ended up meeting Anny at the massage parlor. To know how I ended up there though, you must know how I met her brother Adam first, and to know how I met Adam, I must tell you that I'm a convicted felon.

Living on society's grid doesn't work for sentenced criminals.

"I'm sorry, Johnny," potential employers told me when I was job hunting, "but our company has a strict policy against hiring anyone who has committed a felony." Then the bullshit, the sprinkle sugar they pour on you to soften the rejection. "Keep your hopes high."

Since I was there begging them for a job, the interviewers always wanted to know the details. "What did you do?"

They never cared about what I could do.

Redemption is a myth.

Knowing they weren't going to hire me, I told them all, "I kidnapped my last boss and tied him up in my basement, where I electrocuted him for days using a car battery—not enough electricity to kill him though, just enough to make him squeal. I think I used a Die

Hard. I'm big on irony. Then out of boredom, I slammed a screwdriver through his ear. Don't worry though; he was a real asshole."

Despite my sense of humor, here I was, a broke, jobless ex-con—at least for the moment.

To survive, I was reduced to begging for money, and it only made sense to beg the person that ruined my life.

PRISON DREAMS

Chad Brookings, the all-American quarterback from St. Jude's College, redesigned his body from a pudgy boy to a stoned, sculpted beast. He developed his throwing arm from a flabby uncoordinated appendage to a rocket launcher able to dislodge footballs at missile speeds with GPS accuracy. He did all this, positioning himself to become a professional athlete—every boy's dream—while I walked with my back rubbing the walls of Carthages's Penitentiary, just to reduce the likelihood of being raped.

From my jail cell, the first cage on row one in the F block, I watched Chad outplay his competition every Saturday, just as he outplayed me. I watched him stutter step past linebackers, just like he stutter stepped past admitting to having any involvement in the crime. I watched him juke out safeties, just as he juked out the jury from believing it was his idea. And I watched him strong-arm cornerbacks, just as he strong-armed me to commit the worst mistake of my life.

"How the fuck are you here right now?" Chad asked me when I showed up at the Presbyterian Church in Henry County, a twenty-minute drive from the outskirts of Atlanta.

Now a season veteran professional quarterback, I visited him the day before his season opener.

Being locked in a prison cell, you find yourself remembering everything, every little detail of each day. Without the daily distractions from living a life in the "real world," you naturally recalibrate your focus to the minutia of the prison routine, the schedule. You're consciously aware of each minute, each second even.

This is why it shouldn't be a surprise that I remembered the television announcers speaking about Chad's game preparation during a blowout game. To keep it interesting during the worthless final minutes, the announcers detailed "Chad's winning routine," which entailed going to this the old country Presbyterian Church the night before every game.

"He does this to meditate and be alone with his own thoughts and to remind himself what's really important, telling us integrity and honesty really matters to him," the cap-toothed announcer told the toupee-wearing announcer, who then added more.

"That's right. He's an amazing young man. At such a young age, among all the hype, all the publicity, he reminds himself it's just a game. He even quoted the real Jimmy from the classic Hoosiers movie, telling us, 'It's nice to be important, but more important to be nice.'"

"Great kid, a role model."

It was a hoax.

Chad wasn't alone with his own thoughts in the church.

"Who the fuck is he?" Adam asked while Chad sifted through a handful of hundred dollar bills, counting them all.

This is how I met Adam.

Prison forces you to watch reruns of your life.

The concrete walls and metal bars deny you the "now." They create nothing but a dark void, especially at night. You're left to only think about either your past or your future. Without any external stimulus, you go beyond just thinking. You dissect each and every mistake you made in the past, and you scrutinize each and every move you'll make once released back into society. But this is the ultimate dirty trick that prison plays on you.

Once you're free, you'll realize time didn't stop for everyone else. The people I knew were not denied the "now" like I had been.

The snapshot I had of my mother crying as the guards escorted me away from the courtroom had been replaced by over eight hundred other days of living without me. During these days, she had grown to accept she didn't have a son, especially not a criminal. For her, denying my existence was less painful.

She moved on.

During the trial, people cursed at me, spat on me, and threatened me when I moved around the city. I was denied food at restaurants and grocery stores. I wore disguises to hide from my new infamous publicity.

After leaving prison though, nobody bothered me. Nobody knew me anymore.

They moved on.

They wanted to forget me, all of them—the victim's family, my mother, Chad Brookings. I wanted to forget about me too, to move on as well. But I couldn't. Every application I filled out for a rental, for a credit card, for a job reminded me I was stuck reliving my mistake, told me I was stuck in the past.

Have you committed a felony? Yes.

Since I cannot move forward, I moved backwards instead.

The night before Chad Brookings' next game I went find Chad Brookings and confess my sins. I went to church to come face to face with my past.

I said to him, "I thought this was your alone time."

Chad tossed two brown grocery bags to the floor and then shoved them with feet, forcing them slide away.

"What is this? Are you here to get your revenge?" Chad asked.

Adam backed away from Chad and concealed his money. He said, "Dude, you told me this place was good." Adam eyeballed Chad, waiting for an explanation. I eyeballed Chad, waiting for a confession. "Who is this guy?" Adam asked.

"Nobody," Chad said.

And I said, "He's right. I'm nobody."

Adam grabbed the gun stashed in the back of his pants and showed me his piece. He didn't point it around. He didn't need to. All of us knew the leverage he carried.

"I need help," I told Chad.

"Bullshit."

"I need money."

Chad stood straight up, pushing his chest out.

"Is anyone going to tell me what the fuck is going on?" Adam stayed confused.

Chad told Adam, "It's simple. He's wearing a wire, and you need to shoot him…now."

"No, I'm not," I said, lifting my shirt and revealing my bare chest and prison abs. No wire. "Come on, I just need a little somethin'."

Chad still countered, "I already figured it out. You made a deal to get an early release from prison in exchange for becoming an informant. I bet you loved their offer, bust the all-pro quarterback for narcotics."

Adam raised his gun and asked, "Is that true?"

They both stared at me intensely, both curious, both scarred.

"No," I answered. "I'm here because I'm broke." I turned to Chad, not to argue with him or to blame him but to plead with him. "Chad, honestly. Nobody will help me, not even my own mom. Come on, you know me, the real me. Before all this happened. Remember, we go way back, way before Sarah."

Chad had spent the last years forgetting about me, forgetting about Sarah. He convinced himself that the past wasn't real. Every yard he gained was another yard he made away from the crime. Each step he sank his cleats into the turf made it easier to believe what had happened wasn't real, just a nightmare.

For me, I couldn't run away from it.

My past was a nightmare that I woke up to every single day.

"Don't you bring that shit up. Don't you say another word…not a fuckin' word," Chad said. "Kill him…shoot him," he commanded Adam.

"Fuck you, you kill him cowboy," Adam said and shoved his gun back into his pants. "He's your friend, not mine. I'm not gettin' involved in your love affairs."

Chad and I both walked to the opposite ends of the center aisle.

I told him, "I have nothing, not a cent."

Chad ignored my pleas, just as he ignored them when I was indicted. Instead, he reached out and grabbed both ends of the front benches, positioning himself to launch like a slingshot towards me. "After the shit you put me through, you want me to help you. You almost ruined my life."

"Almost," I interrupted.

He kneeled down into a half-assed runner stance.

"You couldn't just man up… take the responsibility. No, you had to drag me into all that shit," he said.

"Chad, do you not remember? I'm the one that went to prison, not you."

The anger Chad ignited in me was pumping thick through my heart. I could feel the chambers expanding, stretching my muscle cavity, my skin with each thump. My heart reached for Chad, trying to bash his skull, hoping to crack it wide open.

"Are you actually saying that you're the victim?" I asked.

My heart wanted to reach inside him and strangle his soul.

"I can't help it if you were too stupid to get busted like that." He laughed.

He laughed.

HE LAUGHED.

I charged at him, ready to make him feel my pain.

He charged at me, ready to extinguish me.

In the middle of the church, our bones smacked against each other, shoved into each other by our enlarged muscles, driven by our momentum. In the collision, his force outweighed mine. My body sprung off his shoulders. I tumbled backwards as he fell forward on top of my windless body.

I had rehearsed fighting Chad repeatedly while I daydreamed in prison. I had prepared for this moment, lifting weights every day. I had shed my baby fat too, replacing the soft layer with new grown man muscles, rock hard. With my new strength, I visualized breaking my knuckles against his nose, ripping his nostrils in half. I wanted my fingers to hurt because the pain would be a great reminder, a great satisfaction to feel for days. I wanted the bruises to linger, so I could revel in the time when I knocked Chad Brookings the fuck out.

But a want doesn't equal a guarantee.

No matter how hard you work to get that satisfaction, there can be a variable that you were not prepared to handle.

My variable was steroids.

Chad shoved my shoulders flat against the red thin rug running up the aisle. As he pressed down, I felt his strength. Then I felt my manhood evaporate. He was stronger than me, much stronger. He slipped his hand off my shoulder and slammed his left elbow across my nose.

My nose was broken.

Though I was strong, even prison strong, it didn't compete with steroid strong.

Frustrated, I was forced to swallow the blood running from my nose. He elbowed me again and again. I couldn't move. I was trapped underneath him.

I was trapped.

As the steroid-fed punches and elbows rained down on my face, I went in and out of consciousness. Asleep. Awake. Asleep.

I remembered Chad rolling me across the back steps, but I don't remember landing.

THE RIDE, PART THREE

Adam's veins protruded from his face and neck. The drips of sweat migrated from his forehead and tunneled around the veins that held in his pulsating blood.

"Revenge," he said as he tried to rip the steering wheel off the dashboard.

His wide eyes didn't blink. Leaning forward, his anxiety pushed the Civic south, straight down Cleveland Avenue toward what would be almost certain death.

Adam became a common statistic, a typical story. Speed, ecstasy, cocaine, and heroin all consumed him now. The same drugs he dealt to addicts had broken through the paper-thin surface protecting Adam's own vulnerabilities. The chemicals he once used to hide his secrets, his own past, have turned on him and have busted through his weak concealment.

What I remembered from my first meetings with Adam was not an addict, not a man fighting childhood demons. Though he was, he didn't reveal it. Instead, I remembered a focused man who seized opportunity; I remembered a professional criminal.

EASY LOYALTY

I remembered Adam pouring water on my beaten face.

On the church's back steps, I woke up drowning. Instinctively, I rolled over on my knees, coughing water out from my lungs.

"About time," Adam said.

Conscious again, I still felt Chad's elbows slamming my head, thump after thump. Adam crouched down and handed me his water bottle, half filled.

"Do you normally snore dude, cause you were cutting through a rain forest?" he asked.

"Huh."

"Or is that just from an ass whipping?"

Adam offered his hand and helped me stand. Still dizzy, he even carried my dead weight to his yellow Civic.

"I think I'll be okay driving myself," I told him.

"No you won't," he responded.

Adam was the only person to assist me since I committed a felony.

By this time, help from anyone felt foreign.

"No, I'm okay, really," I said.

I felt guilty for accepting his assistance, like I had tricked him into supporting Satan's child. It seemed wrong to prey on his ignorance.

"It doesn't matter if you're okay or not dude," Adam said, pointing to my car, an egg-white Dodge Neon, now severely damaged and immobile. Chad had slashed my tires, broken the windows, stolen the battery, ripped out the spark plugs, cut the cable, and smashed in my doors.

"Thanks for giving me a lift...literally," I said.

Just like that, just for a ride back into town, I was loyal.

Even loyalty is relative.

Driving back into the city, Adam revealed the reason why he was helping me. It was not out of the goodness of his heart but rather out of greed.

"You know Chad wanted to kill you," he said.

I told him, "I kinda got that vibe too."

"No, I'm serious," he said. Adam turned his head back and forth, twisting towards me then back to the windshield; he was watching the road and trying to read my expression. "Chad kept begging me for my gun."

The lumps and discolorations hid my expression though. If he could have read me, he would have known I saw through his bullshit.

He told me, "That's why he bashed up your car instead. I told him I wasn't going let him kill you."

"Thank you," I said. When I spoke, my words merged together. The growing swelling around my jaw destroyed my pronunciation.

"He definitely wants you dead though."

"I guess yurr my herrow," I slurred.

We approached the city fast. My words mutated into moans and grunts even faster. Realizing this, Adam finally announced his motive, getting right to the point.

"So you're desperate for money, huh?"

I couldn't speak anymore. It didn't matter though; the question was obviously rhetorical. Just for confirmation, I still nodded "yes" and groaned, "Dehs puhht ree."

I could have been mad, pissed that he only helped because he saw opportunity in my desperation. I wasn't. I didn't care that he danced around his agenda, pretending to care about me. The point was he still saw opportunity in me when no one else saw anything.

THE RIDE, PART FOUR

When the ride smoothed out again, I saw the familiar street sign for Old Highway 49. When Adam turned right onto this street, I knew the familiar journey we were about to take. I knew we were about to leave the grid and the security and stability that came with it. I knew we were about to reenter a place not listed on a map, where the people who resided there saw death as just another form of currency- same as cash.

I asked, "Jacque's place? Are we making a pick up?"

Adam pushed further down on the gas pedal.

I knew we weren't picking up any narcotics. I knew we weren't seeking revenge against anyone. I just wanted to force him to lie to me, to make sure the battle he was having with his conscious gained momentum, raged on. I wanted his guilt to crack his emotions apart.

Killing Adam or making his emotions implode were my only options for my survival.

He told me, "These fools tried to kill my dad, a fuckin' sheriff. Can you believe it?"

No I didn't believe it.

Why was he driving me to the Jacque's cash house? The only answer that entered my head was that he didn't want to kill me himself.

The white pills were already swimming through his veins. He screamed, "Revenge." He pretended it was meant for Jacque and his other brothers, but I knew it was either meant for his dad or me or for the both of us.

There was a reason why he drove fast towards the cash out, and it was not what I had assumed. Instead, it had to do with a plan. Lucky for me, I knew plans were designed to fail.

NO COUNTDOWN

The next time I met Adam, I tossed three garbage bags of stolen pharmaceuticals in the trunk of his ride, just as he requested.

Until Adam, my life had no purpose, spiraling down towards obsolete. After prison, I searched for a bridge back to a normal life, one where I could live on legitimately. Eventually I understood that bridge didn't exist.

Society never built us a second chance.

Adam, though, did build me a bridge. It just didn't lead back to Normalville; however, it did pay the bills.

"Like I promised." He shoved an envelope of cash in my pants' pockets and slapped me on my ass like a coach does his players.

I worked for Adam now.

Adam's business was stealing and dealing. His main specialty though, what set him apart, was information, criminal intelligence.

His source? His dad, the sheriff of course.

He told me, "My dad likes to brag."

He told me, "He won't shut up about that shit."

This was how Adam became "the connection." Using his dad, Adam knew when and where the raids and stings were going to happen, the details of operations, the status of investigations, who the police suspected, and the names of their informants. Every Sunday dinner, his dad gave him the police's playbook.

"I rarely had to ask him anything," Adam said, "He just volunteer that shit."

Through his dad, Adam bypassed the middlemen dealers and went straight to the supplier. Jacque was part of a handful of immigrants that trafficked narcotics for Guatemalan and Ecuadorian organizations. These guys were expert traffickers, and to be experts in this tradecraft meant they were skilled killers as well. They had to be to defend their lucrative business and protect their trafficking routes and methods against wannabe smugglers.

To excel at this business, a man must be paranoid.

And Jacque's paranoia ranged into the derange. If you complimented him, he thought you were lying and after his money. If he caught you in a real lie, even trivial, he would kill you.

Adam told me, "The story goes that some of his boys planned a surprise birthday party for him. Half his crew pretended that they couldn't go out that night to celebrate; they made up some shit about all having the flu. Of course, what they really did was pull a crazy amount of strippers from Club XO to one of the cash houses, where they surprised Jacque later." Adam shook his head and interrupted himself, "It's a miracle I can tell you this story." He continued, "A few days after the party, Jacque killed most of them. He couldn't handle how well they kept a secret."

"That's got to be a rumor," I said.

"No, that's Jacque."

The art of convincing someone to do something you want is to become that person, not to simply mirror him, but to feel his pain, to believe in his justifications, and to bleed his regrets.

"Dude, I was dumb," Adam said. "I thought I could introduce myself to Jacque, tell him about my connection to police intel and make a deal. I thought he be drooling over what I know." If it weren't for the fact that Jacque thought Adam was a puppet of the police, he would have been shot dead right away. The traffickers' initial belief was that Adam was sent out by the police in an attempt to set them up. Adam said, "That belief saved my ass, dude. They didn't want to kill a cop, especially if they thought they were being watched."

For Adam to gain Jacque's trust, Adam had to jump in the deep end of the crime pool, no time to develop a criminal skill set.

"The only way to prove to Jacque that I was legit was to use my dad's information right away," Adam said. "I made a prediction. I called out one of their buyers, Gary Thomas, telling Jacque he works for Metro. Needing to back up my claim, I told Jacque to have his guys meet Gary at their usual exchange spot—Winner's Car Wash & Wax. Just knowing the spot freaked Jacque out, so I knew when I told him to check out the boarded up Blockbuster across street from the car wash, he'd go ballistic."

Reluctantly, Jacque had his deputy head over to Blockbuster at the same time they were supposed to meet up with Gary. As Adam predicted, cops were inside filming the car wash across the street. Their cameras were wedged between wood boards used to block the windows. Jacque's guy told how he tapped the lens from the outside until the cops realized their cover was blown. The crew went hysterical every time Jacque's deputy imitated the cop screaming "fuck" from inside.

"That wasn't enough," Adam said.

Later, Jacque invited Adam over to one of their stash houses, way out in the country. There, Adam was greeted by Gary, who was blindfolded, gagged, and tied up. He sat on a plastic sheet in the center of the empty living room as the main attraction.

When you commit evil, it's the same as a steel trap door slamming shut behind you as you walk out of your childhood playroom.

Innocence and virginity are the same. Once you lose them, you can never have them back.

They handed him a gun loaded with just one bullet.

"I knew Gary," Adam told me. "I hated him, but I didn't want him dead. Typical story, he was a high school jock. He played baseball. And I was…well…I was nobody, so he fucked with me. He fucked with me a lot. Then he tried to fuck my sister, just about every day. I wasn't having it, so when I saw him at a friend's house party grabbing my sister's ass, I grabbed a rock from the backyard and threw it at him. Big mistake. I missed him and the rock hit his friend Trevor straight on the forehead. Trevor's a big ass dude. Together, they beat the shit out of me. That was the last time I saw him until my dad tells me they busted one of my old classmates for meth possession."

The same as Adam, Gary had gotten in over his head. "It actually woulda been easier if I didn't know him at all, whether I liked him or not," Adam said. They both ended up in Jacque's world. "I was more upset with my dad than Jacque. I couldn't understand why they would risk a guy like Gary, feeding him to this crew, just like that."

Jacque wasn't going to allow dual citizenship between his world and the one Adam's dad protected. Jacque made Adam commit.

"You know when you're nervous to do something like bungee jumping, and the more you anticipate the jump, the more the nerves build. If you don't jump soon enough, you'll have an anxiety attack, so you just jump—no count down. I just planted the gun against his forehead, turned my face and closed my eyes and shot him, no count down."

THE RIDE, PART FIVE

Before the speed hijacked Adam's head, I begged him to stop, to turn the Civic around.

He said, "Don't worry. We're not going in guns blazing."

I played along with Adam, pretending we're going after Jacque still.

Sweat rained off Adam's forehead. Adam was coming apart. As we were about to drive past the too familiar Presbyterian Church, he ground his teeth. He gripped the steering wheel; his eyes watered along with his sweat.

Adam brought the past back to life, at least the past that me and Adam shared.

"Remember Chad, remember how you killed him," he said. "You wanted to kill him, jam a knife through his throat, right."

Now I knew for sure that this ride wasn't his idea, that somebody else was orchestrating a plot against me. Adam had betrayed me. He decided to be an enemy instead of an ally.

The pitch of the Civic's motor shifted from a deep moan to a high buzz as Adam pushed further down on the gas pedal.

"But what did you do instead?" Adam asked.

I replied, "Why, I don't know Adam. Do you mean what we did?"

STEROIDS FOR DOGS

Though Chad didn't give me a cent and kicked my ass almost to a bloody corpse, my surprise visit still paid off.

I made a living stealing for Adam.

He gave me the police's patrol routes and schedules for the evening, along with a list of houses and stores in the unpatrolled areas that did not have a security system integrated with the police department. We prioritized which places would be the most lucrative for us. Lucrative, though, didn't mean the place that housed the most valuable merchandise. If I knew a resident stored a collection of Andy Warhol paintings in the basement, I wouldn't bother breaking in. It would take forever to find a buyer, especially a buyer willing to shop around in the black market. In the meantime, I would be stuck possessing stolen art in the trunk of my car, always just one minor traffic violation from being busted for grand larceny. Instead, we focused on the quick profits—the electronics, the pharmaceuticals, the auto parts. With these products, the buyers didn't ask questions; it didn't benefit them.

Among themselves, thieves demanded ignorance; it was an expectation.

However, I had motives that propelled me to ask questions.

I needed to know more about Chad, and I knew Adam had that knowledge. I had to ask about him.

My fixation towards real justice, towards Chad, wasn't beaten out of me on the church's steps. It lingered with me like a pulsating tumor. Each pulse pushed anger through my muscles. At a random moment, even when I was sleeping, my body flexed, reminding me that Chad had raped my life. I woke up tearing my blanket apart, biting the sheet's fabric until it ripped, fantasizing it was Chad that I was shredding.

Adam told me, "Calm down." He told me, "Take this."

Even when the Zolpidem that Adam shared with me kicked in, I still thought about Chad. "What's he buying from you?...At the church."

Sitting faded in the Adam's parked Civic, he told me, "Roids."

Even Chad's muscles were liars.

"I thought they test for that?" I asked.

"They do, but not the ones I'm supplying. It's an Androgen off-shoot designed by his old college. St. Jude's lab studies it to see if dogs recognize their own strength," he said.

"Dogs? Are you're fuckin' high?"

"I'm serious dude. They want to see if dogs are aware of their own force. They want to find out if dogs know how to hold back when playing with other dogs or humans versus actually fighting them. Basically, they want to see if dogs know they are stronger."

I grabbed another pill and swallowed, washing it down with the Smirnoff Vodka we were sharing. Then Adam told me something else I didn't know. "You know dude, I was hoping you beat the fuck outta Chad."

"Yeah me too."

"You know what that prick said to me the first time we're making a deal? This was when he was still in college. He told me that I better get him a good deal because he's going to go pro. That he can be a long-term client. That I need to think of him as an investment."

Adam saw what I saw.

He didn't see the Chad that those football announcers painted every Saturday and Sunday—a humble and heroic all American role model. He saw an arrogant steroid junkie that thought of himself as invincible and destined for stardom.

I said, "I hate those fucking people. They expect everything to just play out, step by step, like nothing is going to come up and fuck them over and throw everything off course."

"Dude, you cannot plan. At the end, we all die either way," Adam said.

"Okay, it's official. We're fucked up." We laughed.

The more we traded our hatred for Chad, the more I accepted my life in exile. The more we shared vodka and Zolpidem, the more I accepted earning my keep through criminal endeavors. If society rejected me, fuck it—fuck all the employers, landlords, cops, all of the legitimate fools living behind a white picket fence. If the system won't hire me, won't pay me, then I'll steal from the system, wreck the system. When you trap an animal, the animal has no alternative but to attack the one trapping him. I have no alternative but to embrace corruption, theft, destruction, murder.

I told Adam, "I know how we can fuck Chad up and make a real profit."

"I'm in," he said before I even told him the plan.

BETTING ON COLON CLEANSER

I knew God wasn't with me; he wasn't with any of us.

I knew this because he's all knowing. If he is with you, he isn't doing you any favors. To know everything, to see all the answers, you must step away and remove yourself from everything that matters to you.

It was funny; after having delusional episodes of rage, where I released fantasy frenzies against Chad, shadowboxing him, pretending to kill him, and after I was exhausted, and after my muscles were depleted, and I was out of breath, I found clarity. I knew my obsession with Chad led me towards implosion.

To save someone, you must see all the angles, you must see in all directions. If you're on the board playing the game, then you're blind.

Only when I attempted to surrender my crusade against Chad did I have the vision to conquer him—or at least sabotage his life's plan.

"Dude, it's so simple," Adam said.

Before Chad's team, Atlanta, played Jacksonville, Adam met Chad at the old Presbyterian Church, the weekly routine. Except this Saturday, Atlanta was a heavy favorite, more than normal—a twenty-point favorite. Except this Saturday, Adam traded out Chad's steroids for a drug with the street name "Roto Rooter," an industrial-grade colon cleanser. Except this Saturday, Adam and I became sports gamblers, betting big against Atlanta. We didn't even take the points, we betted twenty to one that Jacksonville would upset Atlanta, would upset Chad's grand plan.

On game day, the exceptions to the routine continued. The announcer disappointed the viewing audience, "A big blow to Atlanta, quarterback Chad Brookings will not be dressing for today's game." To calm our nerves, we popped Xanax. "He has checked himself in the hospital," the announcer continued.

"The hospital," Adam said. "What a pussy."

The players lined up for the kick off, but the announcer kept talking about Chad. "I'm reporting Chad suffers from a shortness of breath."

"A shortness of breath, is that normal?" I asked Adam.

The Atlanta players threw their bodies at the Jacksonville team, blocking for their back-up rookie quarterback.

"No, diarrhea, stomach cramps. That's normal," Adam said.

Usually, Atlanta played robotically, emotionless; each player represented a single part of the bigger machine. Except today, they played passionately, aggressively. They played with animal instincts, not mechanically. They played great.

I was sweating. Adam was twitching. We popped another Xanax.

Atlanta dominated, taking the lead into half time. We had jeopardized thousands of dollars, money we couldn't even pay to the several bookies holding our bets. We had jeopardized our lives. We were fucked.

We were not all knowing, yet we still tried to play God. What Adam and I didn't account for was that half of the Atlanta team hated Chad Brookings, much like we did. Without Chad suited up, this game was their chance to prove he was overrated. This moment was their chance to win without him and prove that the narcissistic quarterback was replaceable. Anyone could fill his position.

Their revenge against Chad trumped my revenge against Chad.

That was until news made its way from the hospital to the field.

There was a rumor spreading among the players, and I could tell, anyone watching the game could tell, they turned into zombies. They weren't animals. They weren't machines. They were incoherent, unfocused, depleted. When Jacksonville players slammed their bodies into the ground, Atlanta's players didn't get up.

They didn't fight back.

They didn't win.

They didn't care.

As the game counted down towards the end, the rumor had made its way up to the crowd and eventually to the announcers.

The rumor was Chad Brookings was dead.

The fact was Chad Brookings was dead.

"I'm sorry to report…is this true? Is this not a sick rumor? We can confirm this…" The announcer spoke to his crew working in satellite trucks parked outside the stadium before delivering, "All right, I must inform you that Chad Brookings has passed away."

Adam and I won. We won a serious amount of cash, but we were confused, scared. We didn't hug, high five, or jump up and down. We didn't celebrate.

We were paranoid. Well, I was anyways.

"Do you think?" I didn't even want to ask Adam. It didn't matter though. Speculation wasn't an answer, just ignorance disguised to keep the seat warm until the truth arrives.

Days later, we got our unavoidable answer.

Chad Brookings died from an allergic reaction to the chemical sulfa, which was an ingredient in the industrial strength colon cleanser that we tricked him into ingesting.

How embarrassing? Chad not only died, but he died from swallowing colon cleanser, which everyone now knew about. It's state law that when you're dead, your medical records become public record, even your autopsy report.

WHO'S MORE EVIL

Adam didn't know it, but he introduced me to his sister Anny.

I didn't know which one of us was more evil. Adam, for drooling over the stacks of cash we collected from the bookies at the expense of Chad's death.

He even said, "Dude, we're manipulating more of these games, real soon…soon. This is better than an ATM."

Or was I, for regretting that Chad died? However, it wasn't because we killed him. Instead, I was bummed because Chad wasn't tortured. He escaped pain and went right to death—fucking prick.

Adam misunderstood my solemn demeanor. He actually thought I was morally conflicted over Chad's death. He thought a war between right and wrong waged inside my emotions. He thought the definition of justice was being debated in my thoughts.

"Dude, we didn't have as much control as we think," Adam said. "All you have to remember is it wasn't intentional."

Adam placed two stacks of bills side by side each other, measuring their height and ensuring the lengths match.

"Think about it this way dude, at some point that motherfucker was going to use colon cleanser. Sooner than later bro, cause steroids make you constipated real quick. And most of the cleansers got sulfa in them, so think about that. He was bound to die this way soon anyways." Adam handed me a stack. "Don't treat this like blood money."

"I won't," I said.

I didn't reveal the cause of my depression.

I figured sinister thoughts are best locked in one's head.

Adam told me, "Listen, I want you to head over to this place." He handed me a business card. "Tokyo Spa."

"A massage parlor?"

"Dude, I haven't been, but Jacque's men tell me a massage is their standard service, just the beginning," Adam said.

"Why haven't you gone yet?" I had to ask.

"I prefer whores that make house visits. Something about fucking a chick on the same bed she fucked dozens of other men...I don't know. It grosses me out."

"Well now you sold me!"

"Oh dude, remember to ask for full service." Adam's final instructions.

I'M JUST A CLIENT

Waiting in the white-walled lobby, the Cambodian office assistant offered me another massage therapist.

"Trina's available," she said.

I shook my head "no."

"Rebecca just finished with a client."

I told her, "No thank you."

"Tammy."

"No."

"Laquita, Emily, Stacey."

"No, no, and no."

"How 'bout Anny?"

"Yes. Oh God yes."

In the back room, Anny knuckled in between my shoulders blades.

"You again huh, the no foreplay guy," she said. She dropped a tablespoon of coconut oil on the small of my back. I tensed up immediately.

When the Cambodian assistant walked me to the back room, I saw the man Anny had just serviced walking past—a huge bearded man. He looked like a wannabe lumberjack, draped in a green and blue flannel jacket. I knew he was a wannabe because he was too fat to be cutting trees down. I hated him. There's no way he appreciated Anny, no way.

Anny rubbed the lotion over my ass, letting it melt into the sun-deprived skin. She ran her fingers gently over the hill of my buttocks, parallel with the crack.

I'm just a client, I told myself to counter my addiction for Anny.

When she reached the backs of my thighs, she slid her hand forward under my ass until her fingernails scrapped against my testicles. I shifted. She pinched.

"Don't move," she said. "Don't you fuckin' move."

She pinched harder. I breathed out in moans. My hands clutched the ends of the bed.

She let go. My body deflated, except my dick was hard.

Then with no subtlety, she lodged a finger inside my anus. My legs and back sprung towards the ceiling.

"You like it baby, huh. Tell me you like it," she whispered in my ear.

I could only moan.

She made sure her fingernail carved through me. She said, "Cause this is what a woman feels when a man skips the foreplay, fuckin' rape."

The water in my eyes blinded me.

"You still like skipping foreplay? Huh?"

My body stiffened so much that my bones were ready to break.

"Relationships scare you, huh? Can't handle them huh? Just want to fuck and bail, huh?"

She pulled out and I screamed, "I love you." Then I cried, "I love you so much."

She never said that she loved me, reminding me that I was just a client.

Naked on the bed, I laid vulnerable, watching her clean up like we just committed a brutal, bloody crime. After she finished touching me, she quickly washed her hands, reminding me that I was just a client.

She repeated this every time I visited the spa. I came more and more, demanding that I only see her, no matter how long I had to wait, no matter how many clients she previously serviced. Despite my obsession, she never bothered to remember my name. It was always just "baby," reminding me that I was just a client.

But I convinced myself that I liked that she didn't know my name, that I was just a client.

I liked that she didn't know my history, yet she still knew me, she knew me intimately. She didn't know my favorite color was navy blue, but she knew what scared me. She didn't know I liked my eggs scrambled, but she knew my life was suffocating me. She didn't know I was a Gemini, but she knew regret festered inside of me.

Anny knew I needed to feel pain to then know what pleasure felt like. Every visit, Anny reminded me that I was just a client, but that was okay. She was like the Sun. At just the right distance, she gave me life, but if I got too close to her, she would burn me.

CAUTION

If you ever find yourself in an amazing relationship, one where your highs exceed the most potent dose of heroin, do not try to pump more of that addicting juice through your veins. You will surely overdose.

Caution: If you both have your own places, do not move in together.

Caution: Men, if you don't like to watch romance movies, don't watch them with her. Women, if you don't like sports, don't go to the games with him.

Caution: If you haven't met each other's families yet, don't bother meeting them now.

And Caution: If she doesn't remember your name and you only have sex when you pay her, don't change your arrangement. Keep it that way.

BY THE WAY

The rule is when you win a huge bet against ridiculous odds, you take your winnings and then get the hell out of there, especially if you rigged the game.

Adam doubled down.

Through his dad, Adam learned about a Henry's County Sheriff investigation into an embezzlement scandal, involving several guys. The scandal consisted of a bank employee who was licensed to approve loans, even ones where the recipient was a phony payday company, a company that never actually lent a dime to anyone. The phony company then used the bank's money to pay the "employees" before filing for bankruptcy, before declaring it was unable to repay the bank. These "employees," the ones who actually stole money, included a football referee.

"So I threatened the official. I told him to call the game against Chicago, and we'll find a way to end our investigation of him," Adam told me, real cocky.

"You pretended to be a cop," I asked.

"Yeah dude…well, a corrupt one."

Caution: Don't do business with a psychopath.

Unaware, Adam then changed my relationship status with Anny instantaneously. He told me, "Oh dude. I almost forgot. By the way, you know that Tokyo Spa?"

"Yeah."

"Don't go there anymore."

"Why?"

"It's gonna be raided by the police at any moment," he informed me.

A MEMORIAL TO MY REGRETS

This time, I didn't wait. I busted open the front door and walked straight past the Cambodian assistant.

"Sir, excuse me sir."

I ran down the hall to the back room, "Anny's office."

"Sir, you must check in."

As a rule, the doors didn't have locks.

As a rule, you should always be prepared to see just about anything when you suddenly open a door in a brothel posing as a spa.

Anny was bent over the bed, facing my direction. Her hair hid her face like closed curtains in front of a window. Behind her, the naked fat ass wannabe lumberjack jammed himself inside her, slamming his heavily hairy pubic hairs against her squished ass.

"Get the fuck out," he yelled.

Anny whipped her head up, flipping her hair away from her forehead.

Despite barging in the room, her face told me she was bored.

Her face told me she was stoned.

Immediately, I thought how she would never have to smoke up to fuck me. I might just be a client, but she was at least conscious when we fucked.

I coldcocked the lumberjack straight in the jaw as he pulled out of Anny. Quick advice, if you want to kick a bigger man's ass, fight him when his dick's erect. Unbalanced, the lumberjack stumbled backwards, slipped on a puddle of spilled coconut oil and fell. He slammed his head against the slippery floor.

The Cambodian assistant screamed at me, but she was no longer speaking English.

I grabbed Anny's lab coat. Then I grabbed her arm. "Anny, we got to go," I said.

"Baby, you're always skipping the foreplay." She ran her words together. I went to throw her body over my shoulder, but she stiffened her arms against me and said, "No." When I stood straight up, she shoved her fingers in my mouth, stretching them into my throat. She gagged me. "Don't you dare barf. Take it all in. Keep it all inside you baby." Her strength surprised me. I pulled on her forearm, trying to yank her hand out of my mouth, but she fought back. She jammed her arm further in.

Desperate, instinctive, I pinned my arm back, ready to punch her, ready to brutally release the grip she had on me. But I froze. My mind suddenly shifted to bad memories. I became a statue. The Cambodian assistant's curses faded away. The smell of coconut oil evaporated. I discovered myself serving as a memorial to my regrets.

Until she pulled her fingers out and unplugged all the built up regrets that were percolating within me.

Then I vomited. The Cambodian assistant ran off, still cursing. The wannabe lumberjack stayed laid out on the floor. I kneeled down simultaneously attempting to puke and gasp for air. Anny ran her fingers through my hair, calming me.

When I got everything out of me, when I got passed the dry heaving, when I got my breath back, I told her, "The police will be here any second. They're about to raid this place."

Anny grabbed the lab coat that I dropped. Then she grabbed my arm and helped me up. Then we ran out of there as fast as we could. We left behind the phony front company that acted as our sanctuary from life and entered the real world together, no time to prepare.

SHE KNOWS MY NAME

Sitting in the black Lincoln Continental together, Anny and I watched the police raid Tokyo Spa. The Continental sat towards the back of the parking lot, facing the shopping plaza, where the spa's front door faced us.

We watched the police walk out the handcuffed Cambodian assistant, still cursing.

We watched the police walk out the hand-cuffed wannabe Lumberjack. They covered him in his green and blue flannel jacket.

I turned to look at Anny wrapped in her still-unbuttoned lab coat. I could see the side of her left boob defying gravity. Unable to see the nipple, even the areola, I craved to see her breast. It's funny. The fact that her body was tantalizing covered made me want her bad. If she were completely naked my desire still would have been there, but it would have remained stagnant. However, now I begged for just another inch less of cloth. Because she hid a part of herself, I had put a premium on seeing that hidden gem.

She must have felt my stares, my lust. She adjusted her coat, stretching the ends over her chest. I was no longer a client.

I said, "I'm sorry for killing your buzz."

"Buzz?"

"High."

The police carried computers outside.

"I wasn't high," she said.

The police carried boxes of files outside.

"You weren't. I thought…"

"I was acting," she interrupted, throwing her hands up.

For a split second, I got a glimpse of her breasts before she folded her arms over her chest.

"Acting? For who? For him? The fat ass?" I asked.

The police walked out several half-dressed men, handcuffed.

"Yes, for him, for all my clients, for you Mr. No Foreplay. I give men what they want. He fantasized about raping heavily drugged, barely conscious women. That's what he wants, that's what he gets. I aim to please."

"Why would anyone fantasize about that?" I asked.

"He's ashamed of himself. He knows he offers women nothing, so he doesn't want women to remember him… He isn't much different than you."

The police walked out the hand-cuffed ladies wearing their lab coats.

"Fuck that. Me and him are not the same, not even close," I responded.

"Okay, whatever," she said, dismissing me.

Spectators gathered around the raid, laughing at the Johns and the prostitutes being escorted into the police van.

"You know what Johnny? No. You might not desire to fuck a drugged chick, but you're ashamed of yourself just as much as he's ashamed of himself."

I barely heard her statement.

"You know my name?" I asked.

"Yes Johnny. I know your name," she said. "Even better, I know you prefer me to not know your name. I know you can't handle anyone being close to you. I know you're afraid they'll discover your Big Secret, and judge you for it, and hate you for it."

"How would you know that?"

"The first time you walked in the room, you overcompensated. Your desire to skip foreplay meant you didn't want to develop a drop of an intimate connection with me. Who the fuck just walks in taking off his pants? A pervert trying to hide his insecurities behind a full monty."

Though I was fully dress and she was only wearing a lab coat, I felt naked, exposed.

The police unwound and stretched the yellow and black crime scene tape across the spa's door, marking yet another place I couldn't go to anymore. It was just one spa, one whorehouse, but it felt like the police confiscated my refuge.

THE RIDE, PART SIX

Adam tried to justify murdering me, which was a good thing. It meant he still was wrestling with the idea.

Adam said, "Chad told me everything."

Adam was conflicted, which meant I still had a chance to live, but he was searching for justification, something that would alleviate his pending guilt.

"What'd he tell you?" I asked.

"That you raped some girl."

"It's not true," I told Adam. I'm also telling you that it's not true. "Chad lied." I'm also telling you that Chad lied.

Adam didn't want to believe me. He said, "Bullshit, you went to prison for it, didn't you?"

When did a government document, an entry in a database, a bank statement, a tax return, a criminal history, a credit score become absolute and define a person?

Adam knew better. He dealt with the counterfeiters, the manipulators, the hackers, the identity thieves. At different times and different places, Adam even became those people when needed. He was not one of the many people that never thought about this paradox, about what happens when the system gets it wrong. He knew the system is run by people, by corrupt people. He knew the system is severely flawed.

"And you believe that innocent people never go to prison?" I asked. "And you actually believe Chad over me?"

"Dude, it ain't about what Chad said. You were caught fucking the girl," he said. "I read the police report."

"Adam, you know me."

"If I know you, then how come I didn't know you were fucking my sister? Fuck, you probably raped her too."

When I told the truth, telling everyone I didn't rape the girl, nobody believed me, and they sent me to prison. Now, when I didn't tell anybody about my past, everybody assumed I was hiding a secret and lying again.

And this time they're about to kill me for it.

A BORING DATE

The next thing, we were normal. Anny and I shared a bourbon steak and some Coronas at Applebee's. As if we didn't just escape a police raid, we talked about bullshit— everyday Americana—our favorite movies, songs, cars, you name it. We talked about it, except we didn't talk about the weather. As if Anny didn't just get fucked by a bearded fat ass, she told me I needed a manicure, "Stat."

She asked, "Are you a mechanic? Cause you got all that dirt or oil underneath your nails."

"No, I'm not a mechanic."

Anny did me a favor and didn't follow up with an inquiry about my career.

"Well, you are a very, very dirty lil' boy."

We laughed.

Tonight, for us, superficial conversation in a suburban restaurant chain off the interstate was our oasis. We both had been denied this mundane night for so long. We never got the chance to share time with another person without someone interrogating us. We never got a chance to be ourselves without someone judging us. We never got the chance to sit and speak unguarded without someone trying to use and manipulate us. We never got the chance to just share time, a moment, with someone without being pelted with intrusive questions.

Nobody bothered to be boring around us.

For Anny, the men she knew only spoke to her if instructions were needed to play out their fantasy. For me, nobody wanted me to exist, including my mom.

They all saw me as reminder of a nightmare and preferred if I just killed myself.

Adam was the exception of course, but even he befriended me only as an opportunity to take advantage of my desperation.

"Come on, finish your beer. We're goin' to get your nails done right now," Anny commanded. "Your fingers are grossing me out."

She leaned over the table and kissed me on the cheek. Her gentle lips ran over my body like a warm soft blanket tucking me in on a cold rainy night.

Anny was the exception, no buts.

THE TWELVE STEPS TO A PERFECT MANICURE

The middle-aged Korean lady scraped the dead skin off my fingers, step one. She trimmed my nails, step two; she yanked the lingering ingrown nails from their roots, step three.

"You got me," I said. "I'm that pathetic guy on a date making an ass of himself at the request of the girl, hoping it just might lead to touching a nipple later."

Anny sat next to me, getting her nails done as well.

Following a practical guide, in just twelve simple steps, the tired lady renovated my hands until they were practically reborn. She filed my nails, step four, and then added cuticle oil, step five.

"Um...I already shoved my fingers up your ass, so yeah, I think we're way beyond that," Anny said.

We laughed.

The nail stylists attempted to conceal their disgust for Anny's mouth and hands, but we recognized it. We were veterans in recognizing people's disgust for us.

Refocusing, the stylist soaked my fingers in soapy warm water, step six.

Anny and I eyed each other. Without uttering a word, we communicated. We told each other to be careful through mutual expressions. We told each other to stay quiet, calm. We didn't want people to discover that we were not normal—at least not tonight.

After drying my hands, the stylist rubbed cuticle softener on them, step seven.

Anny asked, "How are you liking it?"

The stylist pushed down on the cuticles, step eight.

"It actually hurts a little," I answered.

Anny said, "Pain means good outcomes. Embrace it."

The stylist buffed the nails, step nine. She removed unwanted oils with acetone, step ten. She applied a primer, step eleven.

If only you could renovate your past in twelve simple steps.

I wished this Korean lady could yank my lingering regret from me like she yanked off my lingering hangnail.

There's so much that people can remake of themselves—their noses, their eyes, their bodies, their moods, their jobs, their cars, their houses, their hair. But you can't remake your memories without lying to everyone and yourself.

The stylist added a topcoat, sealing the polish and the renovation, the final step.

THE RIDE, PART SEVEN

"Chad was full of bullshit," I told Adam. "He didn't tell you about his role, did he?"

If this were a movie, then from a director's perspective, it just made sense. Use a tested formula, which builds up the audience's frustration against the villain by making him hated, making everyone despise him. Then after creating your villain, you have your once victim and now hero seek his revenge on the reviled man, giving your audience their long-desired satisfaction.

As we cruised down Middle Creek Road toward the cash house, toward Jacque, toward my death, I knew Adam attempted to portray me as this villain. I knew his parents, the directors behind the camera, had cast me as the villain, but I didn't know to what extent they had developed me as this character yet.

"Here's the truth Adam," I said. "The night I was caught supposedly raping Sarah...well... Chad was there. Did he tell you that? I bet not."

What they didn't have to make the perfect script was my dialogue.

What they didn't have was my confession that I killed Chad Brookings.

Instead, I gave them the truth, not about the Chad's death, but about the night I was accused of raping eighteen-year-old Sarah Livingston.

"It was Chad's idea actually, not mine," I said. "He was hooking up with Sarah's sister Stacey for awhile."

This must be the thirtieth time I told this story.

"After football practice, Chad asked me to tag along with him over to Sarah's parents' place. The girls' folks were gone and he needed another guy to keep Sarah company, actually distract her while he messed with Stacey. Why not me?"

Adam knew my story was veering from the script, but he couldn't help but listen.

"At the house, all of us were having a blast, getting faded," I told him. "Surprisingly, I have to admit. It was the best time I ever had… well, until of course."

Remembering that night, there was one special moment I hung onto all these years. In one moment, there was a lull between the uncontrollable laugher that me, Chad, and the sisters shared that night. In the middle of the best time I ever had, I mentally stepped away to recognize what it felt like to be truly alive and in the moment. Feeling my cheeks become sore from the constant smile framed on my face, I locked in this memory, not knowing that was the pinnacle of my life then.

"Eventually Chad and Stacey excused themselves and went to the Stacey's bedroom, leaving us—me and Sarah—sitting on the couch in the living room. There, we realized we're feeling each other too, really bad, so since Chad and Stacey had taken their bedroom, Sarah led me to her parents' room."

Adam didn't say a word; he didn't nod, he didn't look at me, he didn't even acknowledge I was talking. Sitting stiff and holding the steering wheel firm, he drove ahead fast down the road, rushing me to me to my death, to a conclusion to this tragedy.

I kept talking, telling him, "There in Sarah's parents' room we fucked. I mean hard, not like porn hard but passionate hard."

Despite Adam's zoned out and indifferent demeanor, I saw the battle going on within him. He didn't want to believe me, but he couldn't deny that I was telling him the truth. It would have been easier for him to believe I raped Sarah.

It would have made all the difference.

"Yes I fucked Sarah."

If I were the true villain written in the script, then he could off me and be the hero.

"But I didn't rape Sarah."

But Adam knew I wasn't the villain. He knew I was the victim all along.

"Before we both climaxed, the parents walked in the bedroom, busted. Their flight to Barbados was canceled, so they returned home."

Plans are design to fail.

Who was the villain? Her dad, who assumed his daughter was a perfect angel.

I told Adam, "He's beating me with everything he can find—hangers, the lamp, books."

Adam woke up and finally spoke. "You didn't fight back?"

"No, not until he grabbed a gun from out of his end table. Before that, I was more concerned with finding my clothes. I didn't want to be running around the neighborhood naked."

Adam laughed.

"When he grabbed the gun, my still-naked ass bum rushed him, knocking him into the wall," I said. "He dropped the gun and I picked it up. Now, yes, I did hold the Livingstons at gunpoint, but only until I got dressed and walked out the front door. It wasn't like they made it sound, where I forced Sarah to fuck me at gunpoint. No, I just used it to get outta there. I dropped the gun on their front porch."

Who's the villain? Sarah, who told her dad and then the police that I raped her, just to keep her perfect angel image in her daddy's eyes.

Irritated, Adam said, "Daddy's little princess. Yeah, I know about that."

"And that's the truth."

Who's the villain? Chad, who denied he was even there that night.

Adam asked, "What about Chad?"

"When he heard me fighting Sarah's dad, Chad bolted, escaped. Nobody saw him."

Adam lifted his foot off the gas pedal, reducing the Civic's speed.

Who's the villain? The police, who never questioned or investigated the Livingstons' story or even considered that I was telling them the truth. That I was innocent.

Who's the villain? My mother, who refused to believe me because it made her feel like she would have contradicted her rape claim against my own father.

After I told my story, Adam refocused and pushed his foot down on the pedal again, speeding the Civic back up. This was my final plea to Adam, asking him to spare my life. At first, I was hoping he found his empathy for me again; that he recognized the brotherhood that we shared.

"Damn Johnny. I'm sorry. I can't even imagine." Then he went back on script, to his obligation to his family. "It makes sense... you know...you killing Chad. I mean the motive is clear, you know dude."

Who's the villain? Adam.

LIFE'S GOT TO BE ABOUT SOMETHING

I took Anny to the traveling circus.

A skinny Filipino man wearing a black and white leotard with the yin and yang emblem plastered on it walked a tightrope hanging fifty feet high. On the tightrope, he adjusted his balancing pole, redistributing his weight, keeping himself center. Where was my balancing pole? Below him, a safety net was stretched out to catch him if he fell. Where was my safety net?

Life's about balance.

Much later that night, Adam and I broke into a university's athletic dorm room and threatened some football players by gun, demanding that they do everything to lose the upcoming game.

Another day, I took Anny out to play a round of miniature golf.

After I made my third hole in one, first through the old red windmill, then a hop over the pond, and finally around the mountain, Anny asked, "How are you so good at this?"

I said, "I guess you have to hit the ball just right. Too hard and your ball will fly by the hole. Too soft and your ball will never make it there."

Life's about precision.

Another night, I crawled through a pharmacy's window with Adam, stealing shelf-loads of prescription drugs.

Anny and I saw a horror movie; we shared popcorn and Twizzlers. When the maniac axe murder appeared out of "nowhere," right behind the helpless blonde, Anny screamed, clutched my arm, and leaned into me.

Life's about surprises.

Adam and I made a movie instead. We covertly filmed an owner of several McDonald franchises. We recorded him fucking one of his female managers in their usual room 314 at the Econo Lodge. Then after we played his performance back to him, we blackmailed him. We threatened to give the film to his wife as an early anniversary gift if he didn't help us out.

Adam said, "One way or another, you're gonna pay for this film. Either you're givin' us some money or your wife gets a shitload of money from the divorce settlement."

He agreed to let us max out his credit cards in exchange for destroying the amateur movie.

At restaurants, Anny and I made fun of the people around us. We pretended to know what they were saying and sarcastically filled in the blanks, mimicking their tone and hand gestures.

Life's about imitation.

At restaurants, Adam and I profiled the people around us. We analyzed their clothes, looking for designer brand names. We analyzed their body language, looking for weakness. We watched them when they sifted through their purses and wallets to pay the bill. We looked to see how much cash and how many credit cards they were carrying—to see if they would make a profitable victim.

I balanced my life between normalcy and criminality, between Anny and Adam. For me, happiness only existed between them. With Anny, we never focused on ourselves. Instead, we kept everything neutral, discussing crucial topics such as celebrities—you know, stupid shit.

"Okay, okay here we go. If Marilyn Monroe was a hot star today, do you think she'll get booty implants to keep up with the big ass trend?" Anny asked me.

"Trick question," I answered back. "Little known fact, but she actually had a bodacious ass."

"You're freakin' hilarious."

"No. The truth is Kennedy loved big asses. Actually, most men like big asses, even back then."

Anny challenged, "Okay, then why only now is it a trend?"

"Simple," I said. "The fashion industry has been dominated by designers, who mainly are gay men. And most homosexuals are not attracted to a big ass."

"Damn, that kinda makes sense in a bigoted sorta way."

With Adam, we focused on surviving off the grid, out of the scope of law enforcement. We discussed crucial topics such as committing murder—you know, fucked up shit.

"Adam, we got to be careful. If we keep threatening guys, someone's going to fight back," I said.

"Then we'll kill him," Adam said.

"Look, what happened to Chad was an accident."

Adam said, "If some dude fights back, then it's on him." He continued, "We all have choices, right?" Then he put it all in perspective. "Besides, you think people will believe Chad was an accident?"

I answered, "No, you're right. Absolutely not."

"I figured you wouldn't." Adam's response revealed he knew more about me than I had hoped. Just like Anny, Adam knew I held secrets without knowing much about the person that hid them. "I hate to tell you this, but we already crossed that line between committing petty offenses and homicide."

Adam's point was dead on, so I quit warning him and agreed with him, recognizing that once again I had passed over a line that I couldn't backtrack across. I said, "Willingness to murder does give us a lot of freedom."

For a while there was happiness in my life, even if it was only as wide as the thin tightrope the Filipino man walked across. As long as I could balance my life, happiness thrived within the fibers of that wire. I had to be precise with both Anny and Adam—never revealing that I enjoyed a normal life to Adam, never revealing that I tortured people to Anny. I wish I could have shared all of me, the whole, with them, but I didn't want to surprise them. I was afraid my other half might scare them away. To hide my inner contradictions, I emitted different personas to each of them. For Adam, I pretended to be an adrenaline junkie seeking his kicks through outrageous crimes versus a man worn down by the increasing brutality that we inflicted against innocent people. For Anny, I pretended that my past never happened, pretended that I wasn't hurting people still—that I wasn't a damage man, but still innocent, neither perpetrator nor victim.

When walking on a tightrope, just the slightest imbalance of weight will throw you off the wire. And the weight of my life was about to drastically shift when my relationships with Adam and Anny evolved. The goal of a tightrope walker isn't to just stand on the wire but to walk, to move forward. Your momentum forces you to move forward regardless. The fact that I even thought I could live my life on a thin thread of wire was the biggest lie I told myself. The fact that I hoped that this life with Adam and Anny could exist in perpetuity reflected my delusional existence.

Life's about change.

IGNORED

No matter how extreme an activity is, if you constantly do something over and over, you'll get bored. Ask a skydiver right before his seventy-fifth jump if he's excited as he was on his first few jumps. Unless he decided to jump without a parachute this time, he'll say no.

For the fourth time, we watched a college football game on the television in Adam's apartment—a game that we rigged. We watched the running back, who we had threatened to kill, purposely drop the ball right before crossing the goal line—fumble.

The announcer shouted, "I can't believe it. The ball just slipped out."

The ability to accept boredom doesn't get enough praise.

The first time we watched a game we rigged, we were nervous, even terrified. The next time, we were excited, shocked at our accomplishment. The third time, we were arrogant, felt like true puppet masters, bragging to each other.

If you can be content in boredom, then you can stop yourself from saying too much.

This time, Adam and I sat way back on his leather couch, half asleep, half faded, half stuffed with pizza.

We watched the quarterback, who we had paid, intentionally throw the ball to the safety, interception.

The announcer screamed, "Who was he throwing to? There wasn't a receiver within ten yards of the ball."

This was when I asked Adam, "Why do you take advantage of your dad like this?"

"Easy money. Ain't it obvious?" he said.

Boredom makes you overthink everything.

"You don't feel bad fucking your dad over like this?" I asked.

"My dad, dude, he's a fucking prick," Adam said.

For most inmates, including myself, prison is an ironic joke. You end up there by doing something stupid because you were bored. Then locked inside your cell, you drown in boredom.

"My dad never gave a shit about me, never," Adam said. "He loved my sister though. He was always with her, always. Me though, he didn't give a fuck."

The quarterback just stood frozen in the end zone, allowing himself to get sacked by a barrage of incoming linebacker, safety—two points.

Adam said, "Did you know how fucked up it is to be ignored by your parent?"

I told him, "Actually I do. My mom disowned me."

"But did she give all her love to your sister right in front of you… all the time?" he asked. Adam didn't give a damn about what I just told him. He was venting, no interruptions. "It's way worse to see what could have been than to never know at all."

Adam's petty complaints irritated me.

I asked Adam, "If you hate your dad so much, then why are you having dinners with him?"

My question and semi-verbal attack forced Adam to sit up, placing his butt on the edge of the couch.

"What do you mean? Adam asked. "He's my dad. It's not like I can disown him."

Not true.

I have firsthand knowledge that family can disown you, literally.

Being disowned by my mom, his answer didn't just tap a nerve, it drilled right through it.

For Adam's family, hate and love are so closely related that they considered them both the same glue that keeps everyone bound together, despite all the conflicts within.

For my family though, we had neither. What I received from my mom was way worse than love or hate. It was nothing.

For her, I was a bad memory.

Every day I reminded her of the man that raped her.

That's right, my dad raped my mom, and my conception was brutality.

My mom never wanted me, wished I never existed. And she would have aborted me if it weren't for the publicity caused by all the information leaks that came from many of the involved lawyers, police, and even doctors that supposedly took an oath to keep this information confidential. Society has no secrets. With everyone knowing about my mom's tragedy, public pressure, the pro-lifers persuaded her to keep the baby, to keep me. I guess I should thank them for my life someday.

I guess I should thank my father too, but he's gone, disappeared. My mom pressed charges against him. Due to insufficient evidence though, my father was released from jail and ultimately was never in my life. Despite the matching DNA that they found in me, the defense attorney argued that she couldn't prove the sex wasn't consensual; she couldn't prove it was rape.

Sitting on the couch with Adam, thinking about my mom, I realized then that I was destined to be disowned by my mom, but Adam wouldn't let me marinate in this revelation. He still had more to tell me about his "sad" relationship between his father and himself.

BREAKING THE ROUTINE

Nobody wants to be in love; the rush is to chase love, not catch it.

Despite keeping our conversations superficial, love caught up to us anyway, and it ruined everything between Anny and me.

"I love you" must be one of the deadliest sentences in the English language. These words kill relationships. They end that retarded happiness that electrifies your senses while you and your soul mate passionately chase each other, learn each other, and feel each other.

I'm not going to lie. When I heard Anny say, "I think I'm falling in love with you, Johnny," bliss overcame me. But when that bliss slowly evaporated off my skin, I felt another kind of love replace the euphoria and develop for Anny. It was a mundane sort of love, like a love for old worn-out sneakers. You're not bragging about them, or excited to lace them up, but you appreciate their durability and longevity.

The words "I love you" should be replaced with 'the euphoria's about to end but I want you to know I'll still be here.'

There's love and then there's loyalty.

And loyalty comes from routines and expectations. Our routine—we always met at the old Trenton Church cemetery. My expectation—she would always be standing at the curb, waiting and lusting for me when I drove up in my Continental. From there, we drove into the crowded city of Atlanta, where its downtown became our hideout. Together, lost among the nameless faces, Anny and I hid from our own lives, our pasts, in all the museums, restaurants, theaters, stores, and hotel rooms that this concrete and steel zoo could provide us.

We never went home together.

Instead, together we escaped ourselves. People will tell you that to love somebody, you must know that person; you must know that person inside and out. Bullshit. Anny and I loved each other for what we offered each other— immunity from our lives, not what we really knew about each other. If Anny had never told me about her family and her past, I would have still loved her the same.

It was Anny's confession, the truth, which stole our passion.

The myth has more power than reality.

The myth will always outlast the truth. For the myth is something we want to believe in, while reality is something we want to forget.

Anny foolishly believed I needed to know everything, and breaking from routine, after telling me she loved me a few days earlier, she suggested, "Why don't we stay here, parked?"

"The graveyard?"

"It's quiet, kinda nice," she said.

Sitting in the car, we had another break from routine. Anny didn't initiate sex this time. She lightly grazed her nails across my jeans covering my thighs. She tilted her head and smiled. But she didn't lean over to kiss me like usual, to suck on my neck like usual. She didn't reach over to stroke my dick like usual. She didn't wrap her legs over my pelvis to grind on me like usual.

She told me she, "felt safe with me."

But she didn't tell me she wanted to fuck me like usual.

Breaking from routine, I plunged my body towards her, kissing her neck. I wrapped my arms tightly around her body, squeezing her, attempting to push the passion out of Anny's soul. But she didn't give in; she didn't release herself to me. Instead, her arms locked up. Instead, she pushed me away. But my pent-up frustration led me to believe she must want to be manhandled, so in a moment, just a moment, just like that, I became the man that everyone accused me of being, but who I adamantly denied I wasn't, never was.

I ripped her blouse. I bit her nipples; I kept her pinned against the side door.

I gave Anny the evidence to doubt me for when the truth would eventually surface and I would need her most.

She screamed.

But I assumed, maybe pretended, that her scream was a scream of ecstasy.

It's commonly known that thirst and starvation can destroy a person's rational thoughts, but did you know that lust also has the same effect?

Anny screamed again, "Please stop."

Then Anny cried. "Stop it."

Then Anny squealed, "Please."

Anny punched me. She clawed me.

But I kept thrusting my weight against her squished body. Though I was crying too, even bawling, I pulled Anny's arms back and worked my tongue down her belly until she moaned out a question I couldn't answer.

"Goddamn Johnny. Why are you doing this?"

Why? Why? I didn't really know why, so I stopped, maybe I actually stopped pretending. I pulled myself off of her and sat back up and said, "I thought you wanted this."

Tears flowed down both of our faces as we fought to keep our past locked inside ourselves. Anny curled into a fetal position, shaking. I just stared at her and said, "I'm sorry."

I was afraid to touch Anny.

Eventually, after some time, she rubbed the tears into her cheeks. She sat up with me, still keeping her distance and said, "No Johnny, I'm sorry." Still fighting to hold back more tears, Anny grabbed my wrist and said, "I guess I don't know how to have sex with someone I love." Then more tears rained down from her bloodshot eyes.

"I don't understand. What's wrong?"

"I'm just not feeling sex right now," Anny responded. "I just need a little time… you know…to adjust. This is new to me."

A night later wasn't enough time. Anny repeated, "I'm still not ready." And again another night later, she wasn't interested. Then another night, she didn't feel me again. Rejection.

After more nights, I felt this wasn't an adjustment period. It was the end. Despite denying me sex, Anny always offered me the constellation prize, telling me, "I love you."

THE RIDE, PART EIGHT

The wind funneling through the open window pushed my words back.

"Do you think I'm just gonna let you deliver me to Jacque's firing squad?"

Adam needed to feel my violence.

"Huh?" he asked.

Adam needed to feel my regret, all of it. I needed him to. If he killed me, he needed to suck in my last breath.

"You can't just do it yourself? You need Jacque?" I asked. "Or is that part of the plan?"

Plans are design to fail.

Adam needed to hear me agonize, "I didn't fuckin' rape Sarah." He needed to hear me scream, "I love Anny." He needed to hear me regret, "But I don't know how to love Anny." He needed to see my regret, see my eyes bulging, see them busting out of their sockets.

If nobody believed me, then everyone would have to feel me.

Shouting against the wave of wind tunneling through the open window, I told him, "You ever heard how revenge is like biting a dog after the dog bit you."

No response.

I continued, "Well, my best friend. I'm your fuckin' dog…once loyal."

Adam needed to take on the pain that was suffocating me.

Even a loyal animal won't just die for his master.

Survival isn't taught. It's built inside our DNA, in all of us.

I leaned over Adam's lap and grabbed the steering wheel.

"Get your hands off the wheel, dude."

Killing yourself while you're speeding down the road to your certain death isn't suicide. It's control.

STRANGERS OR SOUL MATES

All those nights devoid of physical intimacy piled up and weighed Anny and me down, trapping us underneath the built-up frustration. Before we gave up and accepted our love had morphed into a replica of a love between a brother and sister, rather than lovers, Anny scrambled for a solution.

Anny said, "It's like we are stuck in the middle." Anny had this theory. "There are only two types of couples that can have fantastic, toe-curling sex." She then answered, "Complete strangers or complete soul mates." She elaborated, "Soul mates who reveal everything to each other, no secrets." According to Anny's theory, "You're uninhibited when you have sex with a stranger because you don't know each other and you plan on never knowing each other. It's like being invisible; nobody knows your name so nobody can judge you."

"And we're no longer strangers," I said.

"But we're soul mates," Anny responded. "We just haven't shared enough with each other yet. We haven't let go. We haven't fallen into each other's arms, you know."

I wanted to stay on the balance beam, where it was safe. On my right side, I could look down and see my past. On the other side, I saw my future. I saw Anny standing below, holding her hands out to me. Above the crowd, walking on a thin thread, I felt untouchable, but Anny wanted me to fall into her arms and trust that she would be my safety net. Trust she wouldn't assume the worst of me like everyone else in the crowd.

Anny said, "We need to share all of ourselves with each other, you see. Only after we stripped ourselves truly naked, emotionally naked, then we'll be free again, free again to fuck like animals, no inhibitions, no worries, no regrets."

ANNY'S SECRET

First, Anny cried.

Rubbing her shoulder, her arm, I said, "You don't have to do this."

You could see the past boiling up from the dark place in Anny's gut. Her lower abdomen tightened as she fought to restrain her memories from upchucking all at once. She inhaled, and then suddenly dry heaved as her childhood climbed up and out of her stomach.

"I'm serious. You don't," I told her.

"No, I must…We must," she said. "Sometimes we have to go through something painful to get somewhere good, you know." Again, her body contracted and constricted like a deadly hiccup. "Fuck, I'm dizzy," she said, letting saliva run off her lips.

In the back seat of the Continental, I grabbed her shoulders, guiding her to rest on my lap, but she refused and stiffened up.

"All right, I'm just gonna say it before I pass out. Get it over with, you know," she said.

"Okay," I said. I knew right then that we were crossing another line, a line we could never back step over again.

"My dad raped me," Anny spewed. "My dad molested me."

Life is walking from room to room with each door permanently slamming shut behind you. You're stuck carrying all the things you broke in each room, yet you have nowhere to dump the broken items without damaging the room you're currently walking through.

You're just stuck carrying your broken shit.

After Anny confessed, she leaned her body against the front seat.

She was exhausted, depleted. "There. I said it. I'm damaged."

I would be lying if I told you I was shocked. During sex, both when I paid and didn't pay for it, I knew Anny fucked me with demons circling inside her. I just didn't know the origin of these demons until her confession.

"Do you still see him?" I asked.

"Yeah, of course. He's my dad," she said.

Like Adam, she viewed family as an inescapable prison. Soon, I was about to discover why they both shared this same view.

"Is it still going on?" I asked.

"No," Anny said. "Not really. I'm older, smarter now. I'm aware of how fucked up it is now and he knows that, you know." Listening, I wanted to hand her a solution. "Besides, I think he's attracted to little kids. I'm too old now." I could see Anny's nightmares still molested her every night, as if the crime never stopped. "When I was young, fuck, practically a toddler, I thought 'daddy time' was my chore, somethin' I had to do, like brushing my teeth." Anny covered her eyes with the palm of her hands. "I hated him touching me. All day I would dread nighttime, you know, bedtime. Of course that was 'daddy's time.'"

I went to console Anny, but she pushed me away.

At this moment, in these thoughts, human touch disgusted Anny.

"You should see my dad today. He acts like he never did this shit to me; like it never happened," Anny told me. "I just wish I could disappear, you know."

"Why not make him disappear instead?" I suggested.

She said, "You'll kill him for me?"

I nodded yes, no hesitation.

A half smile emerged through her suffering.

"You're sweet, but you can't kill memories Johnny."

Anny forgot an important rule about revelations. When you reveal something, you open yourself to a barrage of intimate questions and advice. You open the door to your innermost room, giving people, including me, an assumption of a "right to know."

"Besides, you'll have to kill my mom too then. She knows all about it," Anny added.

"Your mom's okay with it." That I was shocked by.

"Very much. She made a deal with Dad after she walked in on 'daddy time.'" Anny's arms shook as her eyes bulged and her jawbones tried to break themselves apart. "She told my dad that he can have all the fucked up play dates with me as long as he doesn't touch my younger brother." Now anger gripped my body, tensing all my joints. "For Mom, I was damaged, a lost cause, but my brother—he was still pure. Even more important, our family still needed to appear pure," Anny said. "The family appearance meant more to my mom than my well-being."

"Then why not disappear, for real. Why not?" I asked. "We can disappear together, get lost for good. I can make it happen."

"Quit it, Johnny. You're such a guy. I didn't tell

you all this for you to fix my problem." Anny didn't contemplate an alternative life. "Look, he still provides for me, very well actually. I'm taken care of, better than if I was to go at it on my own." Anny wasn't aware, but I was also trying to fix my problem, kill my memories, bleed them dry. "People have it rough out there... well, you know what I'm saying," she said.

"I'm sorry, but I want to kill him…your mom too. It's fucked up…"

"Hey," Anny interrupted. "Listen. I only told you the worst about my dad." Despite what he did, he was still her dad. "My dad's sick all right, but outside daddy time, he was a good father. He loves me, really."

Loving someone despite being terrorized by that person because you shared his blood was foreign to me, especially to me. I had an urge to break apart Anny's defense of her father's character, to call her out on her insanity, to scream at her and tell her that defending her dad was twisted. But that's the point. Her father was the one who twisted Anny. Her father was the one who turned love into assault, confusing Anny forever, so all I said was, "I'm sorry."

Anny then shocked me again and said, "Besides, my father's a sheriff and my mother's a private detective. If I tried to run away, they'll have the National Guard searching for me. And if you killed my dad, the whole city would be hunting for you."

I stuttered back, "Your dad is a sheriff." An earthquake within me was about to erupt as I discovered how the two tectonic plates that I'd been living on were colliding.

"Okay, I told you all about me," Anny said. "Now tell me your secrets."

THE AFTERMATH OF PASSION

Anny lets me fuck her again.

The key word is "lets."

After divulging her childhood horrors, she thought her spiraling libido for me would reverse. Despite the turnaround, she loved me enough to open herself up to me anyway. She still didn't "want" me—sexually that is—but she loved me.

So I humped her docile body. Hovering over her, I looked into her daydreaming eyes, which stared off towards the corner of the hotel room. I moved my body in and out, repeat. She wasn't dry, but she was barely wet. The drops of fluid scattered through her loins were merely a natural reaction to the physical friction caused from my non-rhythmic stroking. She was not aroused, not in the least, and I was afraid I knew why.

Anny knew how important sex is for a man, for me. She gave me her body. She didn't give me her lust. She gave me her heart. She didn't give me her cravings.

But it really wasn't about Anny.

I don't know if I pulled out or if my dick shrank first, but I did know it was over.

She gave me her sympathy. She didn't give me her desire.

But it really wasn't about Anny.

I didn't give Anny anything, nothing. I didn't share my secrets. I didn't tell her I knew her brother. I didn't tell her I had been in prison. I didn't tell her I killed a man.

I didn't tell her I'd been convicted of rape.

She asked, "What's wrong?"

Everything.

Telling the truth had the potential to free me into Anny's arms, to conquer my past. The truth could complete my conversion. It could turn me from that stranger to Anny's soul mate.

"I can't do it," I said.

But telling the truth risked everything.

"No, don't quit. I know how important this is for you," Anny told me, still staring up at the ceiling. She reached for my dick, ready to stroke it, but it receded beyond the stroking phase. She tugged on my dick instead, trying to resurrect my member.

If she was disgusted by my revelation, if she didn't believe me like everyone else, like my mom didn't, I would have felt completely exiled from love and from life itself—

a dead man.

"Don't worry about it," I said.

I grabbed her wrist, signaling to stop tugging.

If most men had to choose between be sexually wanted and loved, nine out of ten would pick being sexually wanted, and that one guy who chose love would later regret his choice.

Anny rolled over on her side, turning her back towards me. She internalized her failed libido, drenching herself in her own self-loathing. She was frustrated and hurt, and I, the prick that I am, let her absorb all of this responsibility, this blame by herself.

I never shared myself with Anny.

While Anny didn't know how to merge the love that she felt for me with the desire she once had for me, I didn't know how to love—period. I blamed my mother. She never taught me how.

Unlike many women, Anny knew that being loved only equals security to men, meaning that they would have someone there to support them when needed. However, Anny knew that for men, love does not equal happiness. Sex brings happiness to men, not wife or girlfriend duty sex either. I'm referring to animalistic sex, where the woman begs for you with each thrust, where she's half retarded and addicted to you, just wanting to taste you.

For a brief moment, that's what we had. For a long drawn out series of days equaling weeks however, Anny and I lived with the aftermath of passion—when you're just left with love, the loyalty kind.

THE RIDE, PART NINE

Adam overpowered my grip and tugged the steering wheel down to the left, slinging me away. My right shoulder slammed against the door as the Civic spun off Middle Creek and onto Farmington Road. With the wide turn, we almost hit a telephone poll. To avoid the wooden beam, Adam pulled further down on the wheel, swinging the car back on the road, but he pulled it too much. The Civic hopped over the foot-high medium and dove headlights first into the adjacent ditch. Then it flipped onto and over itself several times, down a steep hill carpeted by the yellowish-green grass.

I lost count of the flips after my body smacked into the windshield, shattering it. Propelled from the Civic through the broken window, my body collided with the ground. The momentum kept me tumbling, somersaulting away from the flipping Honda.

I can't tell you when my body stopped rolling. Even after I fell flat, stuck snuggled in the grass, my body still felt like it was in motion, still tumbling.

Looking up towards the sky, a sunbeam broke through the chain of grey clouds and shined directly down on me. Then, I knew I had survived. By now, I knew better than to think heaven would welcome me.

But I didn't know if Adam had survived.

After I pushed myself up and plucked out some of the glass pasted to my arms, I stood up. Amazed—nothing was broken. Amazed—I was alive. I would have relished in my miracle survival if I didn't instantly remember the circumstances of my life.

In the car were those circumstances. Adam's unconscious body sat torqued in an uncompromising position, obvious broken bones. I was jealous though, jealous that Adam didn't have to be awake through the terror of the crash like me. His nightmares remained living only in his sleep.

His face was smashed against the steering wheel.

I slapped him. "Adam...Adam," I said, trying to wake him.

After my third slap, my third attempt, a black wire fell from his armpit. I glided my fingers down the wire to the edge—a microphone dangled from it.

"I knew it. You fuckin' asshole."

I reversed my fingers and retraced my glide, going downward, softly pinching the wire and following it back to its origins—his pants.

A recorder was duct-taped to his inner thigh.

Above on the road, a gas-guzzler, probably a rusted-out pickup truck, sputtered by unaware of the crashed car below, unaware of Adam, and unaware of me. Once again, we were off the grid.

I punched Adam. "Wake up." I punched him again. "Wake up."

Though I assumed the whole time that he was trying to get a bullshit confession out of me, there's nothing like holding the evidence in your hands. There's nothing like confronting a person who ran out of doubt to protect himself.

I hit him again, right in his nose, and he coughed up blood.

He woke up.

He moaned. I mean he really moaned. He kept moaning, really moaning—pain.

He MOANED. He was dying.

And I didn't give a shit. I shoved the wire right in front of his eyes.

"What the fuck are you doing?" I asked Adam. "Tell me."

"I need help," he cried.

I punched him and said, "So do I. Now tell me what the fuck is going on."

"My mom," he cried. "My mom, she knows everything. She knows all the shit we done. She knows WE killed Chad. She knows about you, the rape. Everything. She knows you're fucking Annadale. She knows everything dude."

"How?" I asked.

Adam coughed up more blood.

"How?" I asked again.

Adam moaned "fuck" to push out the pain. Then right before he passed out, he morphed into an adolescent kid who just broke a lamp in the living room by saying, "My mom is going to kill me."

ADAM'S CHOICE

Entropy is basically the theory that everything that has order must eventually fall apart and crumble. Sitting with Adam's broken body, which was trapped inside the totaled Honda at the bottom of a hill, was enough evidence for me to believe in this theory.

Plans are designed to fail.

Yet, knowing things could only inevitably get worse, I still tried to salvage my life.

But then again, that's survival.

I reached into Adam's pants' pocket and grabbed his wallet. He remained unconscious. I reached around towards the back of his pants and grabbed his handgun. He woke up immediately, reaching back to prevent me from taking it, but he was too slow, too weak, too broken, and too late.

That's survival though, fight to your death.

When I first met him, Adam taught me that to get someone to do something he doesn't want to do, you must give him choices. You must give him control, even if it's an illusion.

I placed Adam's gun smack against his temple.

I said, "I'm done playing twenty questions Adam."

He moaned. "Help me, please."

"You can only help yourself Adam," I said, cocking the gun. "These are your choices. First, you don't tell me anything and I put a bullet through your head. Second, you lie to me and I leave you here stranded alone to suffer a slow painful death, where animals will soon gnaw at your wounds. Or third, and I think the best choice: You tell me everything and I'll get you help right away. Your call."

Despite being in agonizing pain, I could see in his eyes that he was proud of me. The teacher had taught the pupil well, even if this wasn't part of the lesson plan.

MY PAST FOLLOWED ME HERE

You might remember hearing about me through the news. If you did, then you'll remember that I was the convicted rapist; the man that news analysts argued should have never been released from prison, free to roam your neighborhood as the boogey man. If you remember this ongoing news story, then you'll remember that I was armed and dangerous. You'll remember I was accused of murdering the football star Chad Brookings—no accomplices. Then you'll remember the media claimed my motive was revenge against Chad for testifying against me in the rape trial. If you kept watching the news coverage, then you'll remember that I became the target of a statewide manhunt after I attempted to kill the sheriff's son by running his vehicle off the road. And of course, you'll remember that the media claimed my motive to kill Adam was to eliminate the key witness in the Chad Brookings murder investigation.

The stories that make the most sense tend to be made up.

Adam confessed, "My mom came up with it." He told me, "She wanted me to help her set you up."

Just as the media knew there must be a motive, I knew Adam's mom, the private detective, must have her motives for wanting to kill me. I assumed she didn't want me hanging out with her son. She didn't want me fucking her daughter. The obvious. But when I asked Adam why she wanted me dead, his answer eliminated the obvious.

He said, "She followed you."

"What? She saw me with you, saw me with Anny, and was curious about me?" I asked Adam.

"No," Adam said. "She found you first and then followed you to us. It was after following you that she found out you were hanging out with me and Annadale."

MOTIVES

After the flipped Civic's wheels stopped spinning, after Adam coughed up some more blood, after I demanded details about his dad's house like the address and security code, after Adam passed out again, after I sprinted away from the crash, after I broke into Adam's parents' home—

which was also his sister Anny's home—I discovered his mom's motivation.

Motives. Everybody has them.

Reputation. Sarah lied to her dad, telling him I raped her because she didn't want to break his heart and ruin her angel-like reputation.

Loyalty. Sarah's sister lied, telling the police she didn't even know I existed to support her sister's bullshit claim and to keep her own virgin image squeaky clean.

Consistency. My mom disowned me, refusing to believe me because she felt that people would then doubt her claim that my father raped her, calling her a hypocrite.

Punishment. Chad lied, telling everyone he wasn't even in the girls' house that night, or with me, because he didn't want to face the same rape charges and barrage of false accusations that I was facing.

I suppose if you can't beat them, join them.

Revenge. I was released from prison and Chad Brookings spontaneously died from colon cleanser months later. Coincidence? The Brookings, both mom and dad being engineers, didn't subscribe to randomness. Instead, they believed in cause and effect. They had relentless faith in the theory that every action has an equal and opposite reaction. They knew his death wasn't an accident. They just knew I had killed him. According to the Brookings, the law of physics required that I should be back in prison serving a life sentence since Chad was dead. According to them, a free Johnny Doherty threw everything off balance, off rhythm, breaking the equilibrium of what's natural.

I didn't belong.

Money. Mrs. Hayden, Adam's mother, located and followed me because Chad Brookings' parents paid the private detective to investigate me, find evidence that I killed their son.

It must have shocked Mrs. Hayden when she followed me and saw her son, a sheriff's son, stealing, dealing, and assaulting people. Then again, if the dad would molest his own daughter and the mom would attempt to kill me, maybe she felt pride rather than shock.

While her initial reaction was debatable, I did know that what most would see as a dilemma, Mrs. Hayden saw as an opportunity.

Remorse. After busting him and confronting Adam for living his dual life, she devised a plan, where all the Haydens could come out as winners despite Adam's previous deceptive practices towards his father.

Mrs. Hayden's plan entailed Adam betraying me; that's obvious. She demanded that her son drive me to the Jacque's cash house under the false pretenses that we were simply going to make a bulk purchase of cocaine. She demanded that he wear a wire and get a false confession out of me; the Brookings were willing to pay for evidence like that.

When we arrived though, Jacque and his men were supposed to execute me. To make this happen, Mrs. Hayden had Adam pay the men ten thousand dollars to kill me, the going rate for murder. Adding motivation for Jacque, Mrs. Hayden instructed her boy to tell this crew that he just found out that I was a police informant.

Notoriety. To make up for conning his father, Mrs. Hayden advised her husband about Adam and Jacque's crew. She would position the sheriff's squad to catch Jacque's men killing me by already establishing surveillance inside and around the house. By capturing the crime in real time, the sheriff could become a hero by seizing a record-breaking amount of narcotics and publicly eradicating these vicious drug dealing assassins from the city's streets.

Trust. The only obstacle to the plan was Anny, but Mrs. Hayden had the obvious solution, of course. She revealed my past to Anny. She told Anny, a victim of sexual abuse herself, that I wasn't just a rapist. I was convicted of it. After trusting me with her confession, after refusing to share my demons, Anny felt betrayed and agreed to be my bait.

For a long time though, I didn't understand why Mrs. Hayden used Anny like that. She didn't need her to execute the plan. My opinion is Mrs. Hayden wanted to strengthen the family's bond, especially after she found out her son was robbing people and her daughter became a whore. The irony was she blamed me for their lifestyles verses her and her husband's parenting.

Plans are design to fail.

Survival. Of course I crashed Adam's Civic because I suspected death was awaiting me in the cash house. Crashing the car was the better alternative. Mrs. Hayden didn't know her daughter like I did. She didn't plan that Anny would have an internal fight raging inside herself. She didn't understand that when Anny saw me drive up in the cemetery, regret immediately would surface to her consciousness, compelling her to warn me that my life was in jeopardy.

Love. After the crash, I needed Anny. The balance beam that I had been walking on had snapped. I was falling, and I needed my soul mate to catch me.

THE MUSEUM OF SIN

The best place to hide from someone looking for you is to hide inside his home.

The Hayden's house symbolized the American dream, literally. The best place to hide your immorality is behind the phony appearance of an upstanding citizen.

A huge red brick two story house decorated with white marble columns in the front represented that appearance, the home of a decent law abiding family.

Of course, it was a façade. Instead the building was the perfect cover up for crimes of molestation and child abandonment.

Tip toeing through the house, I noticed each room was pristinely clean and organized. Too much; the house was so clean it lacked human touch. It felt like I was walking through a house turned museum, where an 18th century family once lived. The house felt haunted, as if this antebellum house and the family that once lived here had earned their celebrity from being brutally murdered in these rooms.

In the silent and the dark hallways, in what appeared to be an empty house, I heard the ghosts of slain children crying. They were the victims of murder, forever stuck here to relive their horrors in the hallways that divided the rooms of hell and purgatory.

Only as I crept up the stairs did I discover that the cries actually came from Anny.

It was easy to trace the sobbing. Once I turned down the upstairs hallway, I knew which room was Anny's. It was the only place where light shined from underneath the door.

When I delicately twisted the knob and cracked open the door, I saw that her room stood out as an exception to the emotionless museum vibe of the rest of the house.

Anny's bedroom was a mess. The room consisted of sloppy piles of all kinds of things stacked everywhere—piles of clothes, trash bags of day old food shoved in the corner, stacks of DVDs, stacks of CDs leaning against her bed, books thrown on each other on top of and underneath a desk, and bottles of lotions loosely spread out on what remained of the open floor.

If you didn't know Anny, you would have thought she was a hoarder. She wasn't. She kept everything in her room, even her trash, because she didn't want to share anymore of herself with her family, not a single item more. Her father had already invaded and taken so much from Anny that she clung to anything that hadn't been touched by him.

Watching through the barely cracked open door, I saw Anny sitting on top of a pile of clothes, just staring out a window next to a lit candle placed on the edge, bawling.

Surrounded by the piles at the edge of the room's mess, I saw what remained of my last vestige of hope to find some type of happiness. Anny sat broken, like a once shattered flowerpot that you glued back together, hoping that when you feed the roots water again, it doesn't leak through all the cracks.

You're hoping that life can break through the depleted compact soil once again.

MOTHERS AND DAUGHTERS

"Anny," I said. "Anny," I repeated. "It's me."

She turned around just in time for me to see tears riding the surface of her eyes.

"Johnny…" I started to climb towards her, but I stopped, leaving my foot lodged between her blue jeans and some sweaters folded inside out. She wasn't excited to see me, nor was she relieved.

"You killed him, didn't you?" she asked. "Didn't you?"

"Anny, stop that. No." I stalled telling her the truth—

once again.

"Quit it Johnny. I don't blame you." Anny said. "It's not like you had a choice."

"Anny, what are you saying?" I asked.

Anny replied, "I'm not stupid. How else could you be here?"

"So you were in on it," I said. "Your mom's plan." For a moment, Anny's eyes went dead. "You figured what? Better Adam than me?"

Anny screamed, "Adam's my brother. He's my family. And you… you…"

"What? What am I?"

Before Anny could answer my question, before I could tell her I was sorry, before I could have a second chance at life, and before I could tell Anny "I love you," her mother shoved a gun right into the back of my head.

"A rapist," Mrs. Hayden said. "A murderer." Her salty chain-smoking voice shocked me more than the gun lodged against my head.

"A liar," Anny added.

Already off balance from standing in the clothes piles, Mrs. Hayden's slight push with the gun forced me to fall over into a pile of trash. When I tumbled, my shirt flipped up, revealing Adam's gun stuffed in my pants. Mrs. Hayden yanked it out and tossed on the bed away from my reach before I even landed.

"You're brave," Mrs. Hayden told me. "You thought you could come in here and rape my daughter and murder all of us. Just like that. Didn't you?"

"I already know I'm a dead man. You won," I said. "I only came here to tell Anny what I should have told her a long time ago."

"Don't you dare. Don't. Don't go tryin' to con my baby girl any more than you already have," Mrs. Hayden interrupted.

Anny then interrupted her mom. "Tell me what?"

"Annadale," Mrs. Hayden commanded, but Anny ignored her mom.

"Tell me Johnny. Tell me," Anny requested.

Staring through the tiny barrel of the gun, I did not speak blatantly. I decided not to say "I love you," at least not directly. Such a strong statement might trigger an impulse reaction from Mrs. Hayden. If I spoke words she designated only for family members, Mrs. Hayden might squeeze her fingers back and kill me while I was sitting in a pile of trash.

Instead, I told Anny, "I finally have an answer to your question."

"Enough," Mrs. Hayden commanded.

"And?" Anny asked.

"We're not strangers," I said.

Anny buried her head into her arms, "Johnny. You can't do this to me, not now. My God, I don't know what to believe."

"Believe the truth Annadale. He's a rapist, convicted," Mrs. Hayden argued. "Believe the truth. Your brother is at the hospital right now because of this man."

"I can't Johnny. I can't. You knew I was falling and you did nothing, nothing! You just let me fall, putting myself out there, exposed. I have to look at motives Johnny. If you cared, you woulda told me then, not now, not with a gun pointed at you," Anny said.

"You must listen to your mother Annadale."

Anny turned her back towards me and stared out the window again.

Mrs. Hayden wrestled her free hand through her jacket's pocket, eventually pulling out a recorder.

"Ahh. I was wondering why you hadn't killed me yet," I said, still begging for Anny's attention, for Anny to listen.

"Yes Johnny. It's time for you to confess your sins," Mrs. Hayden said. "It's time to tell us how you poisoned Chad Brookings."

"Wow, Adam's in the hospital and you're still after the money," I said.

The need to survive, however, refocused me on the gun aimed at my head.

"I'm assuming you don't want me to mention your son's involvement," I said. "Just mine." Mrs. Hayden pressed the red record button. "Why would I lie?" I asked. "The truth is all I have left. Whether I tell you some made up shit or not, you're going to kill me."

I kept thinking about escaping this situation. I thought about lunging at Mrs. Hayden before she could pull the trigger and prying the gun away from her hands, but I didn't know how Anny would respond.

"You are correct. I am going to kill you," Mrs. Hayden said.

"Mom, what are you doing?" Anny reengaged, showing she still cared about me, even if it was minuscule.

I looked to see whether Mrs. Hayden left the safety on, giving me enough time to grab my gun off the bed and fire first, but I still didn't know how Anny would respond.

"Enough Annadale. This man tried to kill...kill, Adam."

The safety was off.

"Your choice is between an immediate death and a delayed death," Mrs. Hayden presented the offer. I thought about pleading with Mrs. Hayden, telling her I would confess to everything and live the rest of my life in prison, but I knew she didn't trust me, especially if Anny didn't trust me. "You can refuse to confess and I'll shoot you in the head right this minute, or you can confess and I'll give you a running head start from the citywide manhunt for you." Ahh, Adam must have learned about giving people false choices from his mother. She advised, "I must tell you. I called my husband, and he and his men are on their way here, and they have strict orders to kill."

Despite knowing that my remaining existence could be counted in seconds, humor entered my brain, thinking about how my life had become a great irony. I had to live with the consequence of a false criminal record for years only to die by a police-sponsored 'off the record" assassination.

"I commend you Mrs. Hayden," I said.

Of course, I knew Mrs. Hayden was lying. There was no way she was going to allow me to depart this house. She was going to kill me right here in Anny's room. The story fit too well. The superhero mom was forced to kill an intruder, who attempted to rape her daughter, only to discover the intruder was the same man who attempted to kill her son and murdered Chad Brookings. Can you make it up any better?

"Commend me?" Mrs. Hayden asked.

I thought that maybe I could save my life by inducing Mrs. Hayden's ego.

"Yeah, after running Adam off the road, I would think that just emotion alone would make you shoot me right away. I mean, like you said, that's your baby boy," I said. "You definitely show impulse control, delayed gratification. You don't cut off your nose to spite your face, making sure you get that evidence for the Brookings first." I finally added, "For that, I commend you."

"You don't even know." Mrs. Hayden took the bait. "When I saw you and found out you were with Annadale, I wanted to put these bullets right through your little testicles. I don't even know if I was thinking about the Brookings offer right then," she said. Mrs. Hayden was too busy reminiscing to realize the lava flow of emotions that started to boil through Anny.

"I bet," I agreed.

Mrs. Hayden just kept talking, kept stirring up the volcano inside Anny. "When I saw you with Annadale at the cemetery, you don't think I thought about how convenient it would be to end your pathetic perverted ass right there, at the graveyard of all places?"

"My God, you knew about me and Johnny the whole time," Anny asked.

The volcano erupted.

"What?" Now Mrs. Hayden was stalling.

"You knew he was a convicted felon, a rapist, and didn't tell me about him until a few days ago."

I added, "But I'm not."

Mrs. Hayden exclaimed, "Annadale, sweetie. I was there, watching you. If anything..."

"Watching!" Anny screamed. Anny stood up and charged her mother, knocking over the candle and tripping over a pile of clothes. Anny screamed some more. "Like you used to watch me and Dad have daddy time."

"Annadale," Mrs. Hayden pleaded.

Anny closed her eyes and swung her fist over and over, knocking the recorder out of her mother's hand. Then she kept swinging and kicking, knocking her mother to the floor between the door's frame.

"Annadale, quit," Mrs. Hayden demanded.

"I hate you," Anny screamed.

Before I could react and pull my legs out from the trash pile and grab my gun, Anny lunged over me, stepping on my back for leverage and onto the bed, grabbing the gun first.

It probably didn't matter though. Despite the beating, Mrs. Hayden held onto her gun the whole time. I would have been shot if I even came close to touching the weapon.

Instead, Anny grabbed the gun in what appeared to seal my death.

Mrs. Hayden and I both assumed Anny grabbed the gun to prevent me from escaping this house. We were wrong.

Anny told her mother, "At least Dad can blame it on a fucked up sickness. You, you though. You chose our family reputation over me, your own daughter. You, you chose money over me, your own daughter."

"Annadale, Listen. Think about my perspective. My husband would rather fuck his daughter than his own wife. How do you think that made me feel?"

"Make you feel…you?"

Anny raised the gun and pointed it right at her mother's left eye.

"Annadale, come on. Don't force me to do this. He's the enemy, not me."

Mrs. Hayden turned the gun on her daughter.

Anny said, "He's not my enemy. No, I know who's my enemy, clearly."

Here I sat stuck in a pile of trash, watching the "ideal" family implode from the built-up pressure caused by covering up their festering demons.

They had turned the guns on themselves.

"Annadale," Mrs. Hayden responded and then she said her last words, "We're family."

Anny pulled the trigger and shot her mother right in the heart, slamming her windless body off her feet and back against the floor.

"We might be family," Anny told her mother, still fighting for breath. "But me and Johnny," she continued. "We're soul mates."

It is highly accepted and well known that mothers instinctively protect their children, even when it means sacrificing their own lives for them. There are countless examples of this motherly heroism throughout history to support this already commonly accepted belief. However, this biological or social occurrence, which most consider the norm, isn't a rule or a law of nature. It has its exceptions, like all the moms who drown their children, or like all the moms who abandoned their babies in a Dumpster each year, or like Anny's mom who pushed her bleeding body up just enough to fire back.

Mrs. Hayden didn't have love for her daughter; she had jealousy.

Though Anny was hit in the stomach, she didn't fall. She didn't take a single step back.

Emotional numbness can give you a lot of tolerance to swallow a shitload of pain.

"Jesus Anny," I screamed.

Anny returned another shot, no flinching. This time, her second shot went through her mother's forehead and killed her.

Only after Mrs. Hayden's body went completely limp, did Anny let go, letting herself crash. I went to catch Anny, but I couldn't find any solid footing on the trash bags underneath me to reach her in enough time. Instead, her weak and vulnerable body landed on another pile of trash.

TOO LATE

Anny was wheezing, lying on her back, but she reached out for my hand.

"I love you Anny," I finally said as my tears dropped down on her cheek.

"Leave... leave now Johnny," was her reply.

I rubbed my fingers through her hair and told her, "No." I told her again, "I love you," hoping if I repeated my feelings they would double in magnitude and become strong enough to conquer our pasts, rip the bullet out of her body, and heal Anny. "We got to get you outta here."

She said, "You're too late." Then she said, "Maybe in another lifetime, one without memories, we can have a chance at life."

More tears slid off my eyes, splashing on her cheek like rain.

"I'm sorry Anny. I should have told you about my past. I should have known that if anyone would have believed me, believed I didn't rape that girl, believed that I wasn't that evil man, it would have been you." Anny tightened her grip on my trembling hand. "I was so afraid that I would lose you. I was so scared you would have nothing to do with me that I..."

Anny cut me off and said, "I believe you."

"What?"

"I believe you."

Her words pierced through my heart like a nirvana lace sword, instantly giving me a peace that I desperately craved.

I collapsed on Anny's chest, crying.

"Johnny. You gotta go. My dad is on his way. You have to leave, leave now," she exhaled, ripping the moment away from me.

"No. No, I'm not leaving again, not this time," I said. "I have a plan."

"You have a plan." Despite the pain, she smiled sarcastically.

"Yes, I'm getting you to the hospital," I said. "We can get through this."

The heat of the moment started to suffocate me. I couldn't breathe. Then it started to irritate my eyes. I couldn't see. Then it started to burn my body. I was sweating. I figured my adrenaline had finally maxed out and burst through my veins, burning me from within.

And I would have continued to think this, if it wasn't for Anny experiencing the same sensation. It wasn't my nerves after all. It was a fire.

The candle that she knocked down when she lunged towards her mother had fallen into a pile of clothes, sparking the quickly breed-ing flames that were migrating towards us.

After we both noticed the fire, she yelled between coughs, "Yes. Burn this bitch down. Let it burn."

I reached under Anny's body to pick her up, but she fought back. "Get out of here Johnny, now."

This time, I fought back and picked her up in my arms and car-ried her like a baby.

"Quit it. You're not dying."

"Johnny, you can't. You can't save me."

When I slowly stepped down the stairs, I heard the approaching police sirens. When I reached the bottom step, I could see the siren's lights.

"They're already hunting me, so just tell them I killed your mom."

When we approached the door, Anny ordered me to put her down. I hesitated, but she shouted with her dwindling energy, "Do it, let me go."

"But Anny," I said.

"Listen, you hear that." The sirens were singing louder and louder. "If you go out there now and start a shootout, you'll be dead and there's no way I'll get to the hospital in enough time."

Anny's soft hands rubbed the tears into my face.

My shirt was drenched in Anny's blood, reminding me that she was bleeding to death.

"No, I can still get you there, now. We just have to go now. Let's go, now."

"Shh, listen baby, just listen to me." The sirens were so loud that they stung my ears. The flashes became so bright that they blinded me. "My dad is sick... fucked up, but he does love me," Anny gently insisted. "He'll get me the help I need, promise. He'll get me to the hospital."

Anny was right.

The police cars breached the Haydens' yard, filing in the driveway, one after another.

She was right again; it was too late.

She said, "Let's focus on getting you out of this hell."

"Okay."

"Go out the backdoor and run through the backyard, pass the pool house and hop the fence. The house behind you is empty right now. The key to the backdoor is on top of the left tire of the boat rack." Out the window, I saw the police forming two lines, guns drawn. "Listen, listen. Once inside, the alarm system is above the kitchen counter, type in code 8081, remember 8081."

"Wait, how do you know this?" I asked.

"Because the Smiths are on vacation and they asked me to watch the house. Go," she yelled. I was about to sprint off when she yelled, "Wait."

"What?"

"Remember, stay there awhile, like days even. Dad's men are probably going surround the whole neighborhood for awhile." As the police approached the front door, Anny gave me her final advice. "Don't run. Don't fight. Just hide."

I said, "I love you Anny," and kissed her before sprinting towards the back.

As I ran, I thought I heard her say "I love you" back. It doesn't matter if she actually said it or not. The point is I knew that she did love me, that she believed in me. As I made it to the back door, I heard the police bust the front door open. As I ran through the back-yard, I heard the flames of the fire consuming the home.

As I entered the Smiths' house, closed the door behind me, and turned off the beeping alarm—8081—all the sirens were muffled. I sat in the dark empty house, afraid if I turned on a light, I would reveal myself to the wandering police. Sitting on the kitchen floor, behind the island, I heard the sirens fade until I heard nothing. Just like that, I went from holding my soul mate to sitting in complete silence and darkness alone again.

INSIDE OUT

Outside, it was storming.

In contrast, inside the Smiths' home I was addicted to the television news. I was glued to the set, watching the nonstop coverage of the statewide manhunt for "Johnny Doherty, the convicted rapist and suspected killer of the sheriff's wife and son." I watched the reporters chase the police, who chased every lead they received about my whereabouts. I watched them break into my mom's house, just after midnight. How horrible? On camera, she was led out of the house by a S.W.A.T. team, sporting her lime-green face cream and a worn out robe. I watched the police encircle the historic Presbyterian Church before the black- uniformed men charged through the doors.

Prior to another raid, I watched the reporters stand behind a mobile command tank and speak about my infamous mythology.

"It appears that John Doherty has a vendetta against Sheriff's Hayden family. This man has not just killed his wife, but tried to kill the daughter and son as well...allegedly."

In an interview with Channel Eleven news, Anny's dad told the reporter, "Know this. We got him on the run, and he's hearing our footsteps."

Only in stillness can a picture come into focus.

All around me, all around the Smith's residence, people were in a chaotic feeding frenzy. And it didn't matter that they were feeding off ghosts and facades. It didn't matter that I never raped Sarah or killed Mrs. Hayden. What mattered was that they believed that I did. The police needed their villain. The reporters needed their story. If you can make a story simple and make it black and white without even a smidge of grey, then you'll have your believers.

Emory University conducted a study once, where they sat fourth graders at a table alone. At this table, the psychologists left a painting of the well-known black and white yin and yang symbol. Next to the painting, they left crayons. Did you know that every single fourth grader colored in the dots with the same surrounding color until the dots completing disappeared?

People don't want complexity. They don't want exceptions to the rule. They either want to hate you or love you.

My addiction to the news wasn't motivated by narcissism. I promise. Instead, I watched to hear about Anny and Adam's statuses at the hospital. Since it wasn't as sensational as the manhunt, their medical updates didn't receive much attention. However, just in case one of them was to die, the news station kept a reporter at the hospital to get the scoop. At least twice a day, to act as a sidebar and intermission to my manhunt, the reporter let me know that, "both Anny and Adam are intensive care but stable." Even better, the reporter informed me, "Both appear they'll make a full recovery."

Knowing Anny was recovering gave me peace in the quiet home. For a brief moment, I enjoyed the solitude and stillness. It was amazing. While sitting in the nothingness that was the Smiths' vacant home, in the eye of the hurricane called my manhunt, I discovered that you can find sanity in a world of madness. That if you could find and live within that dot in the yin and yang symbol, then you just might be able to survive the damaging winds all around you.

INTERMISSION

To get people to quit obsessing over you, force them to deal with a much more serious problem, one they can't avoid.

Staring out the Smiths' master bedroom window, I watched firefighters dig through the debris of the Haydens' home while I ate the last available can of food stored in the house, signifying my time hiding here had run out.

I had to go outside, out there.

Though I found the keys to the Smiths' Audi, though I filled the car up with as much jewelry and electronics that I could stack inside it, though thanks to Mrs. Smith's collection of hats and wigs, I reentered the chaotic world in disguise, though thanks to Adam, I knew which pawn shop and owner wouldn't give a shit that I was on America's Most Wanted List and be willing to buy all of my stolen cargo. I knew that disguises and cash weren't going to save my life. Not just the police were hunting me; just about the whole city wanted me dead.

But I had a plan, and it required me finding Jacque before he and his guys found me. He still thought my dead body was worth ten grand, so the next night I wore one of Mrs. Smith's wigs and drove the Audi towards him, yes, towards the cash house, yes, towards the killers.

Hunger always breaks rationale thinking. It's why the mousetrap works.

Jacque's cash house was far from the city, out in the country. The driveway was three hundred yards long. It wound through and around several trees that had motion sensors attached to them. There were cameras at the end of the road, making it impossible for me to sneak into the house without alerting Jacque.

Unless I chose another path.

Behind the house was a two-and-a-half-mile thick forest stretching out to the interstate. Jacque never anticipated that someone might pull an Audi off the freeway and trek through the muddy woods at night to get at him.

Hunger always breaks rational thinking. It's why snakes attack animals that are bigger than them.

While crawling through the woods on my stomach, I thought about Adam. I thought about how we were almost caught rigging games when the league started investigating how a series of miraculous upsets could occur almost every week. It didn't help that some of the players we bribed and threatened contemplated admitting that they threw games under the scrutiny of the investigation. It didn't help that beloved coach Nelson, who coached the squad with the most bribed players, was the lead advocate for the investigation.

Worried, I asked Adam, "What are we gonna do? They're gonna know it's us...soon."

I will always remember his answer. He said, "We just gotta shift the target dude." I remembered his explanation. "We'll just give the league something more important to investigate."

And that's what Adam did.

Before the team's next away game, before the team walked on their plane at the airport to fly for the upcoming game, Adam paid a baggage handler to place three pounds of heroin in Coach Nelson's checked bag. The moment airport security discovered the contraband, the league's investigation into possible rigged games dissolved and was replaced by the Coach Nelson drug scandal.

Dressed in mud, exhausted, I made it to the back of the house carrying only my memories and Adam's handgun. All I saw was darkness, pitch black. Even the moon was gone. I looked through each window and saw nothing but empty dark rooms.

Were they home?

Maybe they were out searching for me.

I didn't plan for an empty house. I also didn't plan for the internal house security system. How was I going to get inside? If I opened the back door, an alarm was sure to sound.

Plans are designed to fail, especially bad plans.

Hunger always breaks rational thinking. It was why I crawled in mud for two miles without thinking about what I'd do once I reached the cash house.

Frustrated, I slid my back down the siding of the house, until my butt hit the grass. I didn't brace myself for the fall. I didn't prepare for the exhaustion—not just the exhaustion of trekking through the forest, the exhaustion that was my life. I should have known it would eventually overwhelm me, forcing me to collapse, to implode.

Yes, plans are designed to fail, but without them you don't have any hope. That's the real purpose of a plan—hope. Every plan requires hope.

A goal without a plan is just a dream.

Well, a plan without a dream doesn't have a purpose.

And all I could do was hope that there wasn't an alarm connected to the back door, or hope that if an alarm was connected to back door, it wasn't set. These were the only options that I could think of hoping for as I pushed my fatigued and sore body onto my feet.

That was, until another option presented itself, one I could have never planned for.

Jacque randomly walked out the back door alone. Even better, he was unaware of my presence.

It's not about whether you get an opportunity; it's about what you do when you get that opportunity.

"Don't move…don't…don't move," I said.

Jacque didn't turn around, but he still lit his cigarette, even taking a puff.

"I'll fuckin' kill you, promise," I said.

"Then why haven't ya mon?" Jacque asked, taking another puff. Exhaling, Jacque said, "It will be easier to rob my shit if I'm dead, yea? Ain't I just a hassle alive?"

The sweat from my hands mixed with the mud that was already smeared on them. This mixture made me struggle to keep my grip on the gun.

"I'm not here to rob you," I told Jacque.

I was in awe of Jacque's calmness.

There's a certain peace that a man has when he has already accepted his death.

"You haven't killed me. You ain't robbin' me. What ya here for mon?"

I answered, "I'm here to warn you."

Jacque disobeyed my orders and moved, though he did it slowly. He turned around to see my eyes and, I'm assuming, to see if I had a gun like I implied.

"Okay, warn me," he said, and then added, "Johnny."

"Adam offered you money to kill me, right?"

Jacque nodded his head "yes."

"Did he give you explicit instructions to kill me here in this house?"

Jacque replied, "On the property, yes mon."

"Kinda specific instructions, yeah?"

"Maybe, yeah…Yeah mon, I guess so."

Under the starless sky, with my gun pointed at Jacque's chest, it appeared as if the world disappeared around us, leaving just us two. As I explained how Adam attempted to trick him and his guys into murdering me while the police were watching the house, I felt like Jacque and I were living in an intermission to life.

"But what about now? Why ain't no police watching this house now mon? If they know about me, why ain't no arrest, mon?"

"You haven't heard? They got a bigger problem, a manhunt."

Jacque laughed.

People say you're not defined by your obstacles, but how you react to them. The problem with that saying is there are only so many possible ways to react to a particular situation. For example, you don't golf your way out the hood if a golf course isn't nearby or available. Jacque didn't pass on an academic scholarship or corporate job offer to murder fools. Instead, he reacted to abusive poverty by surviving, using any possible means, including killing.

In another life, Jacque and I could be talking about our investments on a golf course.

But this wasn't another life.

After spewing everything about Adam, his family, why they wanted me dead, and why they wanted him arrested, Jacque said the most powerful words. He said in a deep calm voice, "Okay mon. I believe you."

In this moment, in this vacuum where the rest of the world didn't exist, somebody else had listened to me. I didn't care that he was a mass murderer; just like I didn't care Anny was a prostitute.

By now, I realized that prostitutes and murderers are more honest than most people.

"What are you gonna do? Run? Fight?" I asked.

"There's no choice," Jacque said. "They know us now, who we are, and we ain't paid runners, my friend." Jacque finished smoking his cigarette and flicked the butt on the ground. "Now if you'll excuse me," he said, ignoring me, ignoring the gun. "I must prepare." Jacque walked by me, approaching the door. "By the way my friend, clean your gun. There's so much mud inside your barrel. If you pull the trigger, you will blow your hand off."

I thought about asking Jacque for a ride to the Audi, but then I realized the intermission had ended and the show was about to resume.

TIME TO EAT A SNICKERS

Time is on no one's side.

It will run out for everyone, including me, including you, and including the Smith family.

The euphoria that the Smiths were feeling from the wonderful European vacation immediately stopped when they walked inside their home and discovered their appliances, electronics, jewelry, and Audi were stolen.

Time's secret weapon is the "not knowing when it will end."

Just like the Smiths, I became time's next victim when I drove their stolen Audi to their house to discover two police cars parked outside.

Staying at the Smiths' house, driving back and forth to the pawn shop night after night finally caught up to me. I had played too many hands at time's casino. I knew they were bound to return, and they did. If you play long enough, time will always win, guaranteed.

As I was backing in a neighbor's driveway to turn around, I saw a cop walk outside with Mrs. Smith, the violated wife.

Great, I thought. I was about to be caught, even killed, wearing one of Mrs. Smith's wigs. I won't just be consider a rapist, a murderer, the news will definitely add that I was a crossdresser too.

I had hoped that Mrs. Smith wouldn't recognize her own car, but my hope had run out. She pointed at the slow moving Audi, and the cop's eyes followed her finger's direction.

My panic felt her finger.

My panic felt his eyes.

My foot felt the gas pedal as I slammed it.

My eyes saw another cop sprint out of the Smiths' front door through the rear view mirror.

Believe it or not, but when I was speeding away from the Smiths' house and the cops, I reached in a plastic bag of snacks that I bought from a gas station, searching for the Snickers bar that I bought. Facing death or facing prison, either way, I wanted to taste chocolate one last time.

The sirens flashed behind the Audi.

I wanted to embrace Anny one last time.

The police approached me fast.

I bit open the wrapper and took a huge bite. I didn't chew it. I just let the sugar melt in my mouth. I was too exhausted to lead a car chase. I had run out of ideas, plans.

I pulled over and took another bite of the Snicker's bar.

The sirens pierced my ears as they approached.

I grabbed my gun. I was more than ready to aim it at my temple and pull the trigger and say goodbye until I saw that I hadn't yet cleaned the mud out the barrel.

"Fuck."

Well, I lied. I did have one more plan—suicide by police.

But plans are designed to fail.

Bracing for the end, I wrapped my hand around the door handle, ready to run out pointing my gun at the society, ready for the end.

But they weren't after me.

The police didn't stop. They didn't get out and approach me with their guns drawn. Instead, they sped right by the stolen Audi. The target had shifted.

THE STORY THAT MADE
THE MOST SENSE

You might remember hearing about the death squad that declared war on the police. You might have heard that this squad didn't just go after the sheriff but his whole family too. If you remember this story, then you will remember how two men ignited a shootout at the hospital, where they killed the Sheriff's son, including the officer assigned to protect him outside his room.

I will always miss Adam, but survival is an instinct, not betrayal.

If you happened to catch this live on television, then you remember seeing the subsequent shootout unfold, captured by all the media's cameras. If you didn't see the footage live, then you never saw the firefight in the hospital parking lot. Afterwards, the television stations all agreed the footage was too gruesome to air, which meant if you didn't see it live, you never saw a masked Jacque spray four S.W.A.T. members with a modified AK47, savagely wounding them. You never saw Jacque squat behind a shot up black Cadillac Escalade and reach into his black gym bag to exchange his AK for a sawed-off shotgun—the gun police forensics determined blew the sheriff's head into pieces, killing him that night during the fight.

Whether you followed the news coverage or not, whether you even remember hearing about this standoff, I know you never heard about the strategy employed by Jacque.

The police told their story instead.

According to law enforcement, drug-crazed drug trafficking bandits stormed the hospital after they discovered that a man they trusted turned out to be not only a brave informant but the sheriff's own son. The police department's public affairs representative stated during a press conference, "These thugs knew that their lives as free men were numbered thanks to the diligent work of Adam Hayden. They knew they couldn't escape the reach of the law and decided to seek revenge before being captured." The representative said the men "indiscriminately fired rounds at everyone" and called the attack "thoughtless" and "mindless."

The real story is better.

The attack was far from "thoughtless."

Jacque planned the attack. Two of his men did just walk inside the hospital, and they did just walk right up to the officer guarding Adam's room, and they did just start firing like crazy men acting on impulse only. That was the plan. Jacque had hoped that when the sheriff heard dispatch call for immediate assistance, he would rush over to the hospital to save his son, along with all the other officers—all men needed. Once he got what he had hoped for, Jacque's men inside the hospital grabbed random people and used them as shields, just as planned.

Taking hostages forced the police to make a perimeter and to remain outside.

Here's the genius of Jacque. He and the rest of his guys purposely remained outside to flank the police. Since the cops were too focused on the two "mad men" inside, they weren't prepared for Jacque's ambush. From behind police lines, the assassins unloaded on the police, on the sheriff—mass murder.

I will always feel somewhat responsible for the policemen that lost their lives that night, but survival is not a privilege for just a few but a right for everyone, including me.

If you remember this assault on the police, then you remember the following news coverage of the nationwide manhunt for the masked hospital killers. You'll remember the National Guard was activated to assist federal and local agents in this hunt for these notorious killers. You'll remember watching constant breaking news updates telling you the police killed another one of Jacque's men. And you'll remember that the five months long manhunt ended when Mississippi police officers gunned down Jacque after a four-hour car chase on Interstate 10.

But this story isn't about what you remember; it's about what you forgot.

After the infamous gun battle, the police and the media forgot about their original suspect. They forgot about the convicted rapist, the alleged murderer of Chad Brookings.

They forgot about me.

My story wasn't as sensational as a group of assassins waging war on the entire police force. My story didn't include a hero son "volunteering" to go undercover among drug dealers. My story didn't include a twist where the heroic son's true identity was discovered. My story didn't have the heartbreaking moment where he and his father died as a sacrifice for their bravery. My story didn't end with the brotherhood of police eventually getting their revenge and killing the villain, Jacque.

No, my story wasn't as sensational, and it was way too complicated. Who wants to hear about a man wrongly convicted of rape, who's unable to get to job and decided he needed to steal and rig football games to make a living? Who wants to hear about what happens when a daughter, molested by her father with the consent of her mother, grows up? Who cares about a guy living in exile for the rest of his life, a guy living in a duplex that steals for a living and pawns his stolen merchandise?

No, drug dealers going on a revenge-inspired killing spree played better to the news audience. It made the most sense.

Let me tell you from experience. Mundane is the best hiding place in the whole city.

THE THEORY OF FINDING SOMEONE

The next time I saw Anny, she was on the television being pushed out the hospital doors in a wheelchair. Everyone said she looked thin and weak from the ongoing recovery, but I didn't see weakness. I saw a real strength, an inner strength that had finally been freed. The doctors said Annadale suffered memory loss caused from the severe trauma—amnesia. The police backed up the doctors' diagnosis, telling reporters, "Annadale doesn't remember anything from her past, including the night that her mother was murdered and she was shot."

I wanted to see and be with Anny, but so did the whole city.

She became everyone's adopted daughter. After all, she was the ultimate victim, the sole survivor of a family that was systematically murdered. As Anny nursed her injuries, she received money, care packages, condolence letters, and everyone's sympathy.

Though too many people stood in the way between Anny and me for now, I knew that eventually I would reunite with my soul mate.

While everyone has a long memory, everyone's passion dies quickly.

Anny stayed at a gated luxury apartment complex in Suwannee, north of Atlanta. This residence had a security guard stationed in the front twenty-four hours a day, making it difficult to reach Anny. I wasn't discouraged.

Her brother Adam always told me that every single security system is a façade.

He said, "There's always a glitch."

In this case, the glitch was the proximity of grocery stores to Anny's residence. Publix was the only grocery store within a ten-mile radius of the complex, making my plan quite simple—stake out Publix every day since she and everyone living nearby was bound to shop there.

I read a good theory about how to find people. The theory explained that if you want to find someone, you should stay put in one place where there is a high volume of traffic. The idea is that if you stay there for a long enough duration, the person you're following will come to you.

So I waited. I waited all day. Then I waited for days. I got excited when I saw women that looked like Anny, only to realize they were not her. I held my urine for hours, not to miss an Anny sighting. Another day, I had empty bottles ready to avoid that problem. I had the store manager threaten me, forcing me to leave. Of course, I didn't. Instead, every hour, I drove to a new parking space to avoid suspicion. I waited.

And I waited until I saw, yes, finally yes; I saw Anny step out of a white Corolla. At first, I wasn't sure she was Anny. I had been fooled many times before. She wore a blue velvet jump suit, for comfort I suppose, with a dark blue Detroit Tigers baseball cap pushed down tight over her forehead. I assumed she dressed this way to avoid attention. Until I saw her grab a cart and push it inside, I wasn't absolutely sure it was Anny. But when I saw her lean her body over the cart and walked with a lazy limp from her left leg, I knew it was her.

It was Anny.

My impulse was to run inside after Anny, but I didn't.

After days of stillness, sitting in an old Geo Metro, the adrenaline that sprang alive when I saw Anny felt like it was going to erupt and split my heart open. The shock forced me to suck in a deep breath, which pulled a half-chewed Dorito down my throat, causing me to choke and gasp for air. Eventually, I coughed it back up and could breathe again.

After deciding to wait for her to reappear instead of chasing her through the store and risking losing her yet again, Anny finally came outside. She finally reappeared. She pushed a grocery-filled cart across the parking lot. She walked towards the white Corolla. She walked towards me, where I was standing right by it. Patience is a virtue.

A FORGOTTEN LIFE

Our eyes spoke more than our mouths.

When Anny saw me, she stopped. Anny was frozen in time.

"Hello Anny," I said.

"Hi," she returned.

"Do you remember me?" I asked.

"You look familiar, but I'm sorry," she answered. Anny stayed frozen.

"You don't, huh?" I asked again.

"I'm sorry. I don't know if you been watchin' the news. I've been dealing with amnesia. What's your name? Maybe that will help me… trigger something."

There I stood directly in front of my soul mate, the only person other than the late Jacque to believe me, to believe in me. I smiled.

"Maybe it's best that I don't tell you my name," I said.

"It is?"

"Maybe there's a reason you forgot your past," I said. "Maybe it ain't worth remembering."

At that moment, while waiting for Anny to respond, I could hear every single noise around me so vividly. I could hear the engines accelerating and decelerating on the adjacent cross roads. I could hear someone's car brakes squealing to a stop; I could hear a baby crying, a soda can discharging from a vending machine, change falling out of someone's pants pocket. You could hear the off-hinged shopping cart wheel being dragged by the other three.

"Yeah, maybe you're right. Maybe forgetting is better," Anny said.

"Yeah, second chances are very rare," I said. Dejected, I walked away from Anny, saying as I left, "Well, let me just say, I'm really happy you're doing well." I didn't want to corrupt her new life, a new untainted life. Anny was reborn.

Though I was a catalyst to ending her father and mother's horrific rein over her life, I still was attached to that brutal history. Hero or villain, Anny didn't want or deserve to have any connection to her past.

I was halfway between my Geo and her Corolla, when Anny yelled, "Thank you."

I yelled back, "For what?"

Anny left her shopping cart and walked towards me.

"Everyone's trying to jog my memory, like all the time. They're showing me pictures of me and my family, telling me stories about me and them, like they even really knew me or my family. It's annoying."

"Yeah, that sounds annoying."

"Anyways," Anny said, rubbing her hand on my shoulder. "I hope maybe I could run into you again, some time." She stared in my eyes and my eyes stared back. "Maybe I'll get your name then."

Despite our words, the eyes were telling the truth.

"Ahh, names are unnecessary," I said. "Don't you think?"

When she touched me, I had to fight my reflexes, which desperately wanted to wrap my arms around her and hold her tight. I had to stop myself from blabbing, "I love you," and screaming, "you are my soul mate." I had to stop myself from shedding tears. I had to pretend that we just met. I had to hide that I loved Anny.

In a new life, you can't resume where you left off. You have to rebuild.

That's the price of forgetting.

As we separated, she walked back to her car. And I did the same, walking back to my car. Before we disappeared from each other though, Anny had let me know that she still carried a piece of her past.

Anny shouted across the parking lot, "Do me a favor."

"What's that?"

She yelled, "Remember, don't be a stranger."

DESTRUCTION VERSUS TREATMENT

Therapy didn't free Anny from her living nightmares.

Rehabilitation didn't wipe away the stigma of being a convicted felon.

Adjustment, like adjusting her daily schedule to minimize how much she saw her father before his death, didn't stop the ghosts of her childhood from remaining with Anny.

Change, like changing my lifestyle and living off the grid still didn't hide me from the system or from the judgment of society.

And overcoming only meant Anny and I would still have to carry the weight of our past perpetrators with us forever. As anyone knows, you can only climb so high when you're carrying unnecessary baggage. This is why all of the so-called remedies never cured mine and Anny's illnesses. It was only destruction and death that eradicated the viruses that thrived off of our past.

Destruction is a forgotten tool.

In our new lives, we met as strangers again.

Forgetting is forgiving.

In our new lives, our souls remembered each other's love and nothing more because nothing else matters.

Forgetting your past can allow you to see what truly matters again.